HEALTH

SELECT STORES   DALKEY

FUELFOOD

WHOLE FOOD KITCHEN & DELI

Dedicated to everyone I've met along my yellow brick road of life who gave me the heart, the brain and the courage to write this cookbook. You have all inspired me, especially my angels above, Mum and Dad. Thank you. x

STORES

selectstores.ie

SELECT STORES   DALKEY

FUELFOOD

WHOLE FOOD KITCHEN & DELI

THE
FUEL FOOD
COOKBOOK

OLIVER McCABE

MERCIER PRESS
IRISH PUBLISHER – IRISH STORY

SELECT

EST. 1959

SELECT STORES   DALKEY

FUELFOOD

WHOLE FOOD KITCHEN & DELI

ACKNOWLEDGEMENTS

I'd like to thank my partner, Niall, who has stood by me through thick and thin, especially when I was having my Dalkey Diva moments; my family, especially Mum and Dad in heaven, and my siblings Hilary, Leo, Brian and Mairead; all my friends, customers, neighbours and the team at Select Stores Dalkey, especially Eoghan McDermott, Louise Gaskin and Sara Macken, who are always there when I need a hand. Much appreciation to Niall Meehan, who has been such a creative influence in my life; Rosanna Crothers and her husband, Joe, for all the natural daylight for the photo shoot; and the exquisite Dervilla Byrne for her assistance with admin. To Maurice Lawlor, Adrienne Byron, Livia Henderson, Suzanne Doyle, Kate Bentley, Lorraine Oman, Ronan Flynn, Nicole Kamm, Philip Murphy and Dave Flanagan, many thanks for the support. Special thanks to Robert Fisk and Patrick Holford for their wise words, and to John Fahy, Linda O'Reilly, Terry McDonagh and Colm Murphy for their images of beautiful Dalkey. I'd also like to thank the six enthusiasts who got me interested in nutrition and health: Cathy Doyle, Cecilia Armelin, Lorraine Elder, Joan Hanrahan, Olivia Gaynor-Long and Richard Burton. Thanks also to local author Gordon Snell, who taught me the discipline that's required for writing a book!

And lastly, thanks to all the team who have contributed their time and creativity in putting this cookbook together, especially Sarah Liddy, Kristin Jensen, Wendy Logue, Sarah O'Flaherty, Deirdre Roberts, Orla Neligan and Rob Kerkvliet.

FOREWORD

I spend a lot of time travelling around the world teaching the principles of optimum nutrition. But truth be told, there aren't very many places where you can actually eat the foods, prepared in a tasty way, that keep you healthy. One of my favourites is Oliver's Select Stores Fuel Food store and café. It feels like home to me and my stomach, and I always make a detour when I'm in Ireland to have breakfast or lunch, or to stock up with on-the-road supplies. So when I heard that Oliver had written a cookbook giving away his secrets of how to turn the theory into practice with mouth-watering recipes for foods and drinks, I wanted a copy.

One of the great things about these recipes is that they are tried and tested on many happy customers like me, so they are guaranteed to please. Plus they are easy to make, with ingredients you can get in any good health-food store. Even if you don't know exactly what you should be eating for good health, take it from me that these recipes tick all the boxes: low in sugar or sugar free, and high in nutrients, antioxidants, vitamins and minerals.

I happen to be allergic to dairy products. They give me headaches and sinus problems, so I stay away from them as much as possible. But that's not easy in most restaurants and cafés, nor in most recipe books. I also limit my intake of gluten. In Ireland especially there are many people who are coeliac and many more who are gluten intolerant and do much better off wheat, so it's a delight to have so many healthy and well-balanced recipes in one place that are both gluten free and dairy free and taste the better for it.

Well done, Oliver. You've really proven that you can have your cake and eat it too. Thanks for sharing your secrets for healthy and enjoyable eating.

Wishing you the best of health (or *sláinte*),

Patrick Holford

Founder of the Institute for Optimum Nutrition

A Word from Robert Fisk

The 'store on the corner' was what we called it. A windy place with an inch of thick black paint round the windows, it smelled of oil, bicycle tyres, vegetables and moss peat. And the doors of the Select Store were always open and there was always a gale – even in summer – rushing through the shop from Station Road to Tubbermore, a storm of wind only equalled by the gusts above the railway cutting in Sorrento Road. Mrs McCabe was immune to it all – the cabbages on a shelf between the doors, bicycles hanging from racks at the front, the McCabes fuel truck parked on Tubbermore (behind which you could briefly shelter from the wind).

I liked the little stores in Dalkey: the grocer's shop off Castle Street, the electrical shop that fixed old Hoovers opposite Dan Finnegan's – but now the world has to traipse down to Dun Laoghaire to get anything mended (yes, except for shoes at Clegg's) – and the little restaurants that survived (the Guinea Pig) and those that sadly departed (Nieve's). And the 'Select'.

When I was a Trinity student, I lived in one of the single storey cottages at the beginning of Sorrento Road – the one on the right with the big white eagle still over the door, which I bought from a stonemason in Offaly to match the ancient plaster one whose claws still clung to the roof when I first saw the place. The winters then seem cold in retrospect, but the McCabes fuel truck would park round the back of the cottage and the driver would heave a smelly oil pipe over the wall made of railway sleepers and across the postage-stamp lawn into a big green tank that would reek of petroleum for days afterwards. But the little oil-fired motor for the central heating roared away. The fuel, of course, came from Russia and the dangerous Middle East where I worked – and still work – where oil, wealth and poverty and injustice rub so explosively against each other.

I bought Mrs McCabe's peat for the fire, the smell like potatoes, the smoke in the wind scudding across to Maeve Binchy's house opposite. I typed my university thesis in my window opposite Maeve's home – she was writing *Light a Penny Candle* – where she, too, was typing at her front window. When we both finished our work, she formally handed me a first edition of her book as we both stood in the very centre of Sorrento Road. 'In memory of the long days and nights,' she wrote, 'of typing at windows opposite each other.' We admitted later that each of us felt guilty if we abandoned our typewriter before the other turned out the light across the road.

CONTENTS

Dalkey changed, of course, and so did McCabes'. From wind to warmth, from bicycle grease to organic foods and the words 'Health-Health-Health' written above the windows and a seat at the front of the shop where you can drink a latte and feel like you're at the prow of a great passenger liner and watch the *craic* at the multi-crossroads where Dalkey boasts its only five-street intersection. But like Finnegan's on the corner, McCabes' stayed in homely, family hands. Leo and Mairead and Hilary and Oliver – who brought the idea of a health store to the town of Dalkey – now cosset their customers with vegetarian lunches and freshly squeezed juice and homemade just-about-everything and free copies of a health magazine that proves that the 'Select' belongs to the Irish Association of Health Stores.

And so, I'm told, there will be wine at lunch. O Bacchanalia! When Mairead and Steve went off to South Africa not long ago, I suggested to Oliver that he transform the 'Select' each evening into a raving nightclub – and even threatened to call Cape Town to tell his sister the news (playing punk music in the background to give my lie authenticity). But the 'Select's' 5.30 p.m. closing suits Dalkey, a place where health and history and a certain physical fragility come together.

I admit I don't recognise the health experts who drop by for tea, nor wish to read too much in the free health mag in which psyllium husk is recommended for those who suffer from IBS (irritable bowel syndrome, if you really must know). But each time I walk into the 'Select', I'm certain I'll live a little longer, if only because of the vast displays of chocolates with largely unknown names for which I always head (just in front and to the left of the cash desk, if you follow my advice). The prices won't set you back, so Leo and co. need not look at you with a creditor's concern. Ah, let's be frank about it. Family firm. Great food. Clean as a whistle. Not as cheap as the supermarket, but you wouldn't want it to be.

Long life is what matters – along with the memory of all those gusts of wind sweeping through the old shop with ever-open doors. Cabbages, oil and peat. Those were the days …

INTRODUCTION

I grew up in a greengrocers. It never put me off fruit and vegetables – I found it fascinating. Avocados were the new trendy fruit back in the early 1980s, and the trendy vegetable was the aubergine. It looked more like a big black slug to me.

My mum and dad bought Select Stores in 1959. My dad, Paddy, set up a general store filled with bicycles, moss peat, fresh fruit and veg and fuel. He was a strong, generous man. He worked tirelessly setting up local sports clubs and delivered to all the plush hotels and restaurants of Dalkey, including Dalkey Island, Khyber Pass, Silk's and La Baroque. He even went up to Northern Ireland and returned with fresh bread during the bread strike of the 1960s to keep his customers happy.

My dad died in 1980 from a sudden illness, but my mum, Margaret, and my older brothers, Leo and Brian, soldiered on and continued to work full time at the shop. My sisters, Mairead and Hilary, looked after me when we got home from school. We loved making the dinner with Mum once she finished work. Our fun favourites were homemade spaghetti Bolognese and veggie lasagne.

My mum loved to make vegetable soups and stews and lots of nutritious salads in the summer. She made the traditional layered salads with boiled eggs, boiled ham or red salmon, lots of sliced tomatoes, beetroots, salad cream and her homemade coleslaw, which was very popular. Her main courses were often boiled potatoes with sautéed vegetables, cauliflower, turnip, swede or broccoli with roast chicken, roast beef or even fresh mackerel or crab from the local Bulloch Harbour. A lot of our friends adored her cooking and would call in when they could for a bowl of soup or roast beef salad sandwiches, always leaving with happy faces.

So you could say that this was where my love for food began. I did my school homework in the kitchen, so I was continuously consumed by foodie sights and smells.

When I returned from Australia and the States in 2001, I made the decision to work full time at Select Stores. At the time it was a struggling greengrocer. My mum was ready to retire, my sister Hilary was having her first baby and my brother Leo was working hard with his business, the neighbouring fuel merchant. So this was my golden opportunity to reinvent Select Stores. It took me three years to get there.

In 2004 we transformed Select Stores into a dynamic health-food store selling a large range of organic produce, healthy foods, skincare and household products alongside a juice bar and wholefood café. I also returned to college, the Irish Institute of Nutrition and Health, at the weekends to study nutrition, to support me in my role at the shop. Studying nutrition enabled me to offer advice and tips to customers and clients while they were food shopping or eating or sipping. Dealing with and meeting customers on the shop floor is an integral part of my working day, and above all has taught me that every customer is an individual. Learning about their nutrition and food requirements is invaluable to me and adds to my knowledge of the ever-transient food world ... and sometimes I also look after the odd baby while Mum and Dad get the shopping done.

Sadly, my mum died just before Christmas 2012. It was a very tough time for us as a family. She was such an inspiration to us as an individual who cared not only for her family but also for her community. She lives on in all of us today.

In 2015 we reinvented Select Stores once more, as we wanted to keep up with the health-food trends, or as I say, 'keep one step ahead of the posse'. We now have a new fresh wholefood kitchen and deli, which we called Fuel Food (hence the name of this cookbook). And Mum and Dad are still looking down on us each day from their picture in our café.

Recently I have noticed that a lot of our customers are trying to make healthy food for their families on a budget and stressing out over complex recipe books and ingredients. So with this book I'm bringing healthy wholefoods back to basics for you. Here you will find my favourite simple, flavoursome, healthy recipes with lots of nutrition tips and advice that I have accumulated over the last fifteen years while working around the world and living and breathing Select Stores in Dalkey. I have been listening to what our customers want and keeping my big ear to the earthy ground to keep you fuelled every day.

I hope you enjoy and have fun with this Fuel Food cookbook.

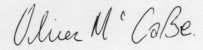

THE CORNERSTONES OF GOOD NUTRITION

We are all biochemically individual when it comes to nutrition, although all of us have the same basic requirements when it comes to eating in a way that promotes good health. Ideally, we should have three meals a day with two snacks in between to keep us going throughout the day. Food combining is a way of putting meals together so that they provide complex carbohydrates, essential fats, protein and dietary fibre, with adequate water for hydration. All the food-combining recipes in this cookbook support the body with brain function, energy production and optimum nutrition to help keep you focused and fuelled all day long.

I have set out the cornerstones of good nutrition below. Get these right and your body will thank you.

WATER

We all learned in school that the human body is two-thirds water, so hydration is critical for flushing toxins from your body and carrying nutrients to your cells. Water is so important that our bodies require more of it than any other nutrient. The recommended eight glasses per day assumes that you are getting at least two to three cups of water daily from fruits, vegetables, soups, etc., which all count toward your eight glasses of 'water' each day.

When you don't take in enough liquid, it can make you tired and irritable, and it can affect your exercise performance too. Keeping a water bottle nearby will encourage you to drink, and many people find that it helps if they keep track of their intake. Make a habit of drinking a glass of water as soon as you get up in the morning. If you don't like plain water, try sparkling water.

Protein

This amazing nutrient is needed daily and many believe that protein, health and fitness go hand in hand. It's true – your body requires protein for many different functions. Protein is basically the building block that you use to produce natural chemical reactions to assist the digestion, absorption and metabolism of foods.

GROWTH

Your body requires protein to build, recover and grow its structures and tissues, such as muscle, hair, nails, etc. Remember, protein is the solid building block for body tissue.

HEALTHY IMMUNE SYSTEM

Protein helps you produce antibodies that make up your defence system and help protect you against colds, the flu and other health issues.

DIGESTION

You need protein to produce enzymes for proper digestion, absorption and energy metabolism.

PROTEIN

ENERGY & VITALITY

Protein is used to produce energy and may assist with the metabolism of other nutrients, like fats and carbohydrates.

PERFORMANCE & RECOVERY

Protein helps to increase and maintain energy production and recovery for active people and athletes. It may also help reduce the effects of injuries and overall recovery.

MOOD & BEHAVIOUR

Protein helps your body produce hormones that can affect your mood and behaviour for the better.

The secret is to incorporate a good variety of vegetables and high-quality, ethically farmed fish and animal sources of protein into your diet and divide them into small, frequent meals. The protein content of each food type varies, although the key is to keep it balanced and as healthy as possible. Eating fresh, organic and unprocessed foods will help deliver good nutrients to your body. Some great protein sources are:

- **Legumes:** beans, chickpeas, lentils, pinto beans, black beans, mung beans, bean sprouts, etc.
- **Seeds:** hemp, chia, flaxseed, sunflower, pumpkin and sesame.
- **Nuts:** almonds, walnuts, Brazil, cashew and pistachios, to name a few.
- **Eggs.**
- **Lean meat:** chicken and fish, for example.
- **Dairy:** milk, yoghurt, cheese, etc.
- **Vegetables (all) and avocados.**
- **Seaweeds and algae:** kelp, wakame, nori, spirulina, etc.
- **Grains:** quinoa, millet, amaranth, rice, rye and wheat.

· ·

FIBRE

Fibre keeps your digestive system healthy and contributes to other processes, such as stabilising glucose and cholesterol levels. It is recommended that adults eat 25–35g daily. Here are some ways to increase your dietary fibre intake:

- Choose hummus instead of cheese when snacking. While cheese has no fibre, a quarter cup of hummus, which is made from chickpeas and sesame seeds, provides nearly 4g.

- Swap a serving of meat for a serving of beans. Half a cup of beans has 5–8g of fibre, depending on the type, while chicken and beef have none.

- Munch on nuts. Adding a quarter cup of nuts can give you an extra 2–4g of fibre. Almonds have the most, but peanuts and walnuts are also good sources.

- Eat your vegetables. You can boost your fibre intake by 4–8g by remembering to eat half a cup of cooked greens or a couple of raw carrots.

- Go with whole grains. If your rice is brown, a cup will give you about 4g of fibre, but if it's white, it only has 1g. Other whole grains like oats and quinoa also provide lots of fibre.

. . . .

ESSENTIAL FATS

Healthy fats are important to help you feel fuller for longer and they help aid the essential functions in your body. However, when eaten in large quantities, especially before exercise or work, they can make you feel heavy and they can slow down digestion, making it difficult to absorb nutrients as fuel. The fat found in fish (omega-3), nuts, seeds (such as flaxseed and chia seeds) and avocados are more essential to bodily function than the saturated fat in cheese, fatty meats or deep-fried foods. Try to limit your intake of hydrogenated and saturated fats (fried foods, takeaways, ready meals), which only increase fatigue and sluggishness.

. . . .

CARBOHYDRATES

The main nutrient that fuels your body is carbohydrates. The more 'whole' or complex the carbohydrate is, such as brown rice, quinoa or wholegrain pasta, the longer the fuel will last. Carbohydrates are found in:

- All types of grains, such as brown rice, wheat, oats, bran, millet and quinoa.

- Nuts, seeds and wholegrain pastas.

- Most vegetables, but especially starchy vegetables such as sweet potatoes, peas, beans, legumes and corn.

Fight the sugary food cravings

Many of us would like to cut down our sugar intake, but it can be difficult to resist the craving for sugary, sweet foods. Try the tips below to reduce your sugar intake.

- Eat plenty of fibre. Fibre makes your body feel fuller quicker during meals, and keeps you feeling full for longer. Replace refined sugars with fruit and white bread with wholewheat choices. Add extra vegetables to your meals every day.

- Sleep at least eight hours each night. Sleeping less may make you crave sugary foods and drain your energy during the day, making you burn fewer calories.

- Eat several small meals a day – breakfast, lunch, dinner and two snacks rather than three big meals. Don't skip any meals during the day. Skipping meals may cause you to overeat at your next meal. Your body compensates for the skipped meal earlier in the day.

- Snack on finger foods between meals and avoid foods that are high in carbohydrates. Sugar causes mood swings and quick changes to your energy level. Your energy level peaks after eating a high-carbohydrate meal, but dips shortly afterwards, leaving you hungry before your next mealtime. Try carrot and celery sticks.

- Avoid eating when you are angry or emotional. Go for a walk or attend a yoga class.

- Participate in regular exercise or play a sport that you love and look forward to. This will get you over that 'couldn't be bothered' attitude. Your body produces endorphins when you exercise, releasing serotonin, the feel-good hormone, into your bloodstream. These hormones also inhibit food cravings and burn extra calories throughout the day, making it easier to compensate for a mistake when you slip into a food craving.

Sugar alternatives

Sugar raises your blood sugar quickly, leading to the inevitable 'sugar highs' followed by a crash. So what are the alternatives?

○ Stevia is a herb that is much sweeter than sugar, with insignificant calories.

○ Xylitol is an unrefined plant sweetener with a very low glycaemic load and can be used in cooking and baking.

○ Barley malt syrup is as sweet as sugar with the same amount of calories, but raises blood sugar more gently. It also contains B vitamins and minerals.

○ Maple syrup is delicious and sweet, with just over half the calories of sugar. It is made from the sap of maple trees and contains small amounts of vitamins and minerals.

○ Honey has fewer calories than sugar, but is almost as sweet. It is often antibiotic, especially manuka honey, which is made with pollen from the tea tree.

○ Blackstrap molasses is a by-product of sugar refining. It's very high in iron and has fewer calories than sugar. However, its sweetness is due to the same molecules as sugar.

○ Fruit concentrates are lower in calories than sugar and raise the blood sugar more gently. You can get fruit concentrates as liquids or spreads, often organically grown.

○ Fructose is marketed as a natural alternative to sugar, but it's actually manufactured from industrial glucose. It has the same amount of calories as sugar, but does raise blood sugar very slowly.

• •

EATING BEFORE AND AFTER EXERCISE

The best foods to boost your store of energy are rich in complex carbohydrates, such as quinoa, brown rice, wholegrain pasta, fruits and vegetables. When it comes to activity, it's important to time meals right so that you use your fuel most efficiently. Eating two hours before any activity or exercise gives you time to digest and top off the tank. Don't forget that refuelling after activity is equally important, ideally within 30 minutes. Balancing meals with carbohydrates, adequate protein, and fruits and veg will provide premium energy to fuel your body.

FOOD COMBINING

Food combining provides nutrients, essential fats, complex carbohydrates, fibre and protein at each meal of the day so that your body receives optimum nutrition. For example, in the recipe for **Fresh Bircher Muesli with Mixed Berries and Flaxseed** on page 71, you gain essential fats from the flaxseed, complex carbohydrates from the oat flakes and protein from the natural yoghurt. This provides fuel for your body to give you more energy over a longer period of time until your next meal.

. . . .

SLOW DOWN

When you eat too quickly you don't digest your food properly, which can lead to indigestion. Eating quickly also means it's easy to eat too much, as you don't give your body a chance to tell you that it's full.

Eating meals in courses is one way to slow your pace. Taking smaller bites helps too. If you're eating food that needs to be cut up, like a piece of meat or chicken, cut as you go. Practise putting your utensils down periodically during the meal, stop to sip on water or simply take a little break. Work towards making your meal last for at least 15 or 20 minutes.

. . . .

STORE CUPBOARD INGREDIENTS

Almond butter: A store cupboard necessity that's delicious, versatile and full of minerals – an all-rounder ingredient.

Apple cider vinegar: An alkalising vinegar made from apple cider that's good for digestion.

Buckwheat flour: A gluten-free flour that makes perfect pancakes.

Cacao powder: Cacao (raw cocoa powder) is full of antioxidants and fibre. I use it a lot in healthy treats.

Chia seeds: Small, dark seeds that are high in fatty acids essential for brain health.

Cinnamon: Cinnamon is one of my favourite spices, as it regulates blood-sugar levels, giving energy over longer periods of time.

Coconut aminos: A soya-free, coconut-flavoured protein sauce that's perfect for dressings. Make sure to choose a gluten-free brand.

Date syrup: A dark, intense, fruity syrup and plant sweetener that's ideal for healthy snacks.

Edamame beans: These tasty young soya beans are mostly sold frozen. They're low calorie, have no cholesterol and are full of protein and minerals.

Grapeseed oil: A reasonably priced oil that's ideal to use for high-temperature cooking.

Himalayan fine rock salt: My no. 1 store cupboard essential. You'll see it everywhere in this cookbook. This pink salt is the purest salt around and contains eighty-eight known trace elements.

Honey: I prefer to use local honey, as the antibacterial level is higher. The closer it's made to you, the better.

Liquid aminos: A soya protein sauce that's ideal for savoury dishes and dressings. Make sure to choose a gluten-free brand.

Maple syrup: A caramel-like plant sweetener that's perfect for baking.

Natural coconut yoghurt: Use instead of creamed coconut or coconut milk for creamy sauces without most of the fat.

Nutritional yeast: Non-dairy, cheesy-flavoured yeast flakes that are ideal for pesto and sauces.

Olive oil: Find your perfect olive oil, be it extra virgin, organic or local. Small producers rule. Olive oil is best kept for low- to medium-temperature cooking, or for salad dressings.

Organic canned tomatoes: Organic canned tomatoes taste better and give more flavour to dishes.

Organic chickpeas: Organic chickpeas are usually bigger, plumper and rounder than non-organic ones.

Organic coconut oil: This is one of my favourite oils to use, especially for high-temperature cooking.

Organic eggs: I prefer cooking with organic eggs for quality purposes.

Organic oat milk: This makes food creamier and can be better for digestion than cow's milk.

Organic rapeseed oil: A locally produced oil that's perfect for high-temperature frying.

Rice wine vinegar: Make sure you buy rice *wine* vinegar instead of rice vinegar.

Sesame oil: A cooking oil derived from sesame seeds – ideal for wok frying.

Shoyu sauce: An intense, full-bodied, flavoursome soya sauce. Note: this contains gluten.

Spelt flour: A flour that's similar to wheat but has fewer calories, more plant protein and is easier to digest. It's fantastic to bake or cook with and is readily available.

Sumac: A tangy, lemony spice used instead of lemon juice or to season spicy dishes. It's especially yummy in homemade hummus.

Tahini: A creamy sesame seed paste. Use light tahini for hummus and dark tahini for dressings.

Tamari sauce: A soya sauce that's savoury to the max. Make sure to choose a gluten-free brand.

Unsalted butter: Contains no salt and is good for baking or frying at high temperatures, as it is a solid fat (or non-hydrogenated) and has a higher smoke point than salted butter.

Unsalted stock bouillon cubes: Easy-to-use, salt-free and yeast-free cubes for making stock. Make sure to choose a gluten-free brand like Kallo or Marigold.

Unsweetened almond milk: Another favourite milk alternative that's full of minerals.

White wine vinegar: A tangy vinegar made from good-quality white wine for dressings.

GLOSSARY OF NUTRIENTS

Throughout this book, I have mentioned the vital nutrients that each recipe has in abundance. Here is a brief glossary in case you're wondering what's what.

Allicin is a component of garlic that is released once the garlic is crushed or minced. It has very high antibacterial levels, which supports the fight against germs within the body.

Antioxidants help prevent free-radical damage to your body's cells. Free radicals cause oxidative damage that may lead to disease. This can be caused by bad diet, alcohol consumption, smoking, chemicals and even pollution in the air we breathe. Colourful fresh foods such as berries, apples, carrots, greens, nuts and seeds are high in antioxidants.

B vitamins are eight water-soluble vitamins that are vitally important for brain function and adrenal health. These vitamins are best consumed through food in the morning at breakfast to keep you focused and relaxed for the day ahead.

Beta-carotene is a red-orange substance with antioxidant properties that may protect against free-radical damage and oxidation of cells. It's found in carrots and sweet potatoes.

Bromelain is an enzyme that digests protein within the body. It may also help to reduce indigestion or inflammation within the digestive tract. Pineapples are high in bromelain.

Calcium builds and maintains bones and teeth, and supports muscle and heart function. Calcium is particularly abundant in kale, dairy products and sesame seeds.

Dietary fibre aids the digestion of food through secretion and also helps to clean up the digestive tract. Dietary fibre is abundant in apples, broccoli, parsnips, spinach, beans, whole grains and bran.

Essential fats are vital for brain, heart, bone, joint, muscle, cardiovascular and skin function. They also play an important part in regulating cholesterol. They are found in fish, nuts, seeds, avocados and olives.

Folic acid supports one of the B vitamins, B12, in maintaining the body's cells and nervous system. It also may regulate inflammation within blood vessels. Beetroot and wheatgerm have lots of folic acid.

Iron is very important to human life. It helps to transport carbon dioxide and oxygen back and forth from the lungs to the body's tissues. When blood is deficient in iron, it may cause anaemia.

Lycopene is a phytochemical with antioxidant properties that may protect against free radical damage and oxidation of cells. It's found in tomatoes and red peppers.

Magnesium helps to regulate calcium metabolism and plays a large part in maintaining bone, muscle and brain function. Magnesium is found in seaweeds, green vegetables, nuts and seeds.

Manganese is an essential nutrient that supports blood-sugar control, energy production and thyroid function. It is found in nuts, whole grains and green leafy vegetables.

Protein (plant or animal) cannot perform its vital function of fuelling the body and repairing the body's tissues without the support of the essential vitamins and minerals we consume every day through a healthy diet.

Selenium is a highly powerful antioxidant that works well with vitamin E in foods to support the body against disease and viruses. It's particularly abundant in Brazil nuts.

Vitamin C is a water-soluble antioxidant that helps replace oxidised cells from a bad diet or alcohol consumption. Vitamin C is particularly helpful when the immune system is weak and it works well with fat-soluble zinc to remain in the body to be absorbed rather than excreted.

Vitamin E is an antioxidant that is particularly important to eradicate any cell toxins from the body, such as heavy metals. It also supports your immune system during stressful times and is vital for heart protection. Vitamin E is found in all nuts.

Zinc is an antioxidant that's particularly important for men, as deficiency in zinc may lead to prostate cancer. Zinc is also important to help absorb vitamin C within the body and is vital for skin health. Pumpkin seeds are particularly high in zinc.

ALLERGENS

It is an EU requirement to display all allergenic ingredients used in the production or preparation of food in restaurants, etc., to alert consumers who have an allergy, sensitivity or intolerance to any of the fourteen listed allergens: gluten, peanuts, nuts, milk, soya, mustard, lupin, eggs, fish, shellfish, molluscs, sesame seeds, celery and sulphur dioxide. The relevant allergens are mentioned in each recipe in this book, indicated by the symbols shown below.

If you have any special dietary requirements, each recipe will tell you what food category it's free from and what allergens it contains. There is also an indication of whether a recipe is vegetarian or vegan.

SOY Contains Soya	F Contains Fish	V Vegan
M Contains Milk	MD Contains Mustard	GF Gluten Free
E Contains Eggs	G Contains Gluten	DF Dairy Free
P Contains Peanuts	SH Contains Shellfish	NF Nut Free
C Contains Celery	N Contains Nuts	SF Sugar Free
SE Contains Sesame	VG Vegetarian	

When a recipe says it's sugar free, it means it contains no refined or processed sugar, which has a very high glycaemic load. When a food or recipe is low GL, it means it has a low glycaemic load of complex, 'whole' carbohydrates or complex, naturally occurring sugars. Low GL foods stabilise your body's blood sugars at a slower rate than high GL foods, such as refined sugar, leading to a steadier supply of energy over a longer period of time. Low GL foods benefit brain and athletic performance and also alleviate hunger, leading to a more controlled, balanced diet.

NB: coconut is a drupe not a nut and is generally not a problem for people with tree nut allergies. So any recipes using coconut are marked as nut free. However, if you do have a nut allergy and are concerned about this please consult an allergist before trying any of these recipes.

BREWER'S YEAST

ORGANIC CASTER SUGAR

ORGANIC SOFT BROWN SUGAR

ORGANIC COCONUT PALM SUGAR

RAW CANE SUGAR NEVER TASTED SO SWEET

biona

DURA WHOLE CANE SUGAR

Maldon SEA SALT FLAKES

IRISH ATLANTIC SEA SALT

taste

Irish sea salt
Handcrafted

PRO FUSION

HIMALAYAN ROSE PINK CRYSTAL SALT COARSE

PRO FUSION

Sel Marin Vintage

HIMALAYAN ROSE CRY

MORNING WAKE-ME-UPS

After you get up and shower in the mornings and before you eat food, it's lovely to wake up your digestive system slowly. It too sleeps at night, slowly detoxifying the body, which is why we usually need the loo first thing in the morning. So here are some easy-to-make warm drinks that will kick-start your digestion before you have breakfast, preparing you for the day.

EASY
DIGESTION

🍴 **SERVES: 1**

Ingredients
1 teaspoon raw mother apple
cider vinegar
A squeeze of lemon
250ml warm water

Raw mother apple cider vinegar is a purer, more potent form of apple cider vinegar. You can buy it in your local health-food shop. High in vitamin C. Low GL.

Pour the cider vinegar and lemon juice into a cup. Top up with the warm water and stir slowly. Sip and sip and sip until it's all gone!

AUTUMN
WINTER MORNING

🍴 **SERVES: 1**

Ingredients
½ teaspoon manuka honey or
local honey
¼ teaspoon ground turmeric
¼ teaspoon freshly grated root
ginger
A squeeze of lemon
A sprig of thyme
250ml warm water

This is delightful if you're feeling poorly on an autumn morning, as it's fantastic for the throat and respiratory system. I love using turmeric, as it has an amazing anti-inflammatory effect on the body. High in vitamin C. Low GL.

Add the honey, turmeric, ginger, lemon juice and thyme to your favourite cup, then add the warm water and stir slowly and lovingly until infused. Sip slowly and relax.

SPRING
SUMMER MORNING

🍴 **SERVES: 1**

Ingredients
½ teaspoon elderflower cordial
¼ teaspoon honey
A sprig of fresh mint
250ml warm water

I love making this during warm months to slowly activate digestion with fresh mint and delicate tones of elderflower, which is known to lower blood sugars. Low GL.

Add the elderflower cordial, honey and sprig of mint to your favourite cup, then add the warm water and stir slowly and lovingly until infused. Sip slowly in your cosy chair and relax.

CHEAP
COLONIC

🍴 **SERVES: 1**

Ingredients
1 tablespoon golden linseeds/
  flaxseeds
¼ teaspoon honey
250ml warm water

A college friend of mine, colon hydrotherapist Donna Boissiere, recommended taking this warm drink first thing in the morning. It's full of goodness and fibre to shift everything along. High in dietary fibre and iron. Low GL.

Add all the ingredients to a blender. Blend for 15 seconds, until it turns milky. Pour into a glass and drink quickly.

SMOOTHIES AND JUICES

In 2004 I opened a fresh fruit and vegetable juice bar as part of Select Stores, working with local suppliers and farmers and using organic produce where possible. We have gone through a lot of recipes over the years. Some have stayed and some have gone, but here are a few of my favourites, plus my advice and tips on juicing and smoothies.

Any of the juices and smoothies in this chapter can be part of a juice cleanse. When you do a juice cleanse, you should feel more energetic and your digestive system should feel lighter. You may also experience better skin tone and a general feeling of alertness. The end result is overall well-being.

When our bodies are confronted with colds and the flu, run down and exhausted, fresh fruit and vegetable smoothies and juices provide incredibly effective protection. Overall, freshly made smoothies and juices are alkalising, cleansing, energising, healing and highly nutritious, because the ingredients are largely raw and still contain a lot of their life force (the nutrients present at the time of picking).

But what is the 'green' in a green smoothie or juice? Basically, this is any leafy green that can be wrapped around your finger and is safe to eat. These greens will provide you with vitamins, minerals, fibre and the best blood-builder of all – chlorophyll. Your body digests smoothies and juices much faster than normal foods, allowing all the goodness to get to your bloodstream quicker.

Add fruits, nuts and superfoods to this and you have a recipe for success. Superfoods have exceptional benefits due to their high concentration of nutrients that support and increase the immune system's ability to work better. Just remember that when you begin taking superfoods, such as spirulina, start with small amounts and increase them over time. Also, I don't recommend adding superfoods such as wheatgrass, barleygrass, spirulina or chlorella to your juices or smoothies if you're pregnant, as they can cause nausea.

I use a tablespoon of apple cider vinegar diluted in a basin of hot water to wash my fruit and vegetables. This removes any dirt, wax, preservatives and pesticides from conventional fruit and vegetables. Remember that the more local the produce is, the better. The further away the produce has come from, the more preservatives and refrigerators are required to keep it fresh. Always ask your local shopkeeper or supermarket where the produce is from and if they don't know, don't buy it.

TIPS

TIP 1

Most juicers these days are powerful so you can add your ingredients whatever way you like, but you may need to chop ingredients to a smaller size to fit the juicer, rather than add them whole. Take your time! They say the slower you go the more fibre you'll require. Leafy greens such as spinach, parsley or kale may need a hard fruit or vegetable, such as apple, to assist while juicing to produce more juice rather than pulp for the bin. Always check your bin, as when it is full the pulp can end up in your juice. Always try to use your pulp for the compost heap, for the best garden in town.

TIP 2

Soft fruits like pineapple, mango, papaya, kiwi and banana should only be blended in a blender and not juiced. If you juice them, they will only end up as pulp in your juicer bin, wasting your time and money.

TIP 3

Always make your juices and smoothies fresh and drink them slowly, not fast, so that your digestive system can process and absorb the nutrients properly and easily. If packaging them, use a flask or a good plastic or glass bottle to store. Fresh juices should always be consumed within an hour as the nutrients deplete quickly. Refrigerate smoothies for up to three days only. Always shake before use. Add a squeeze of lemon or lime as a natural preservative.

TIP 4

Always have your juices and smoothies for breakfast or lunch, not for dinner, because they could ferment with your evening meal and make you feel unwell, as your digestive system is preparing to rest and is not fully functional.

TIP 5

Have fun creating your own recipes with your friends, parents or children. Just make sure you clean up after yourself.

SUPERHERO
GREEN JUICE

 SERVES: 1

SF GF DF NF V

Ingredients
4–5 small apples
1 medium cucumber
1 floret of broccoli
1 very small piece of fresh
   root ginger
1 lime, peeled
⅛ pineapple, peeled and
   cubed

Try this super-green smoothie to increase your energy levels for four to five hours. You can drink it slowly at breakfast or as a mid-morning snack. It will help you get through your long day and from desk to dinner. High in vitamin C. Low GL.

Juice your apples, cucumber, broccoli, ginger and lime. Put all the juice and the pineapple into a blender and blend for 15 seconds. Pour into a glass and serve immediately.

SUPERMODEL
GREEN JUICE

 SERVES: 1

C SF GF DF NF V

Ingredients
220g fresh spinach
20g fresh curly parsley
4 small apples
4 sticks of celery
1 medium cucumber

All this goodness on the inside will have a positive effect on the outside, because feeling fit, healthy and energised really shows. Take antioxidants, for example. They are present in fruits and green vegetables and are essential for younger-looking skin. Folic acid is present in leafy green vegetables, which helps to keep hair and nails strong. High in vitamin C and magnesium. Low GL.

Juice the spinach, parsley, apples, celery and cucumber. Pour into a glass and serve immediately.

FLU FIGHTER
JUICE

 SERVES: 1

Ingredients
4 carrots
3 small apples
Small piece of fresh root
 ginger
1 medium beetroot
2 oranges, peeled
1 lime, peeled
Pinch of ground turmeric

This has probably been our most popular juice at Select Stores since 2004 – the feedback from customers is always positive. It's a winner for the cold months of the year. The ginger and turmeric make it powerful stuff for the respiratory system. High in vitamin C and folic acid. Low GL.

Juice all the ingredients in the order listed except the turmeric. Juice the harder produce first, leaving the softer produce until last, then stir in the turmeric. Pour into a glass and serve immediately.

THE ANTI-CANCER
QUEEN

 SERVES: 1

Ingredients
2 small apples
2 carrots
2 sticks of celery
200g fresh spinach
25g fresh curly parsley
¼ cucumber
1 small floret of broccoli
1 small beetroot
½ lemon, peeled
1 small finger of fresh root ginger
25g alfalfa sprouts

The only reason I call this juice the anti-cancer queen is because it's a very special recipe loved by customers, such as Andrea Crowley, Anna Gallagher and Andrew Clarke, who have just finished chemotherapy or radiotherapy. They find it effective and re-energising. You should only drink it a few times a week, as it's potent. Take it easy to begin with – make small amounts and sip it slowly. It's packed full of goodness and nutrients, including alfalfa sprouts. Not enough people eat or grow alfalfa sprouts. Considering their many alkalising health benefits, it's time to consider adding them to your diet. High in vitamin C. Low GL.

Juice all the ingredients in the order listed, except the alfalfa sprouts. Stir the alfalfa sprouts into the juice, then pour into a glass and sip gently.

· FUEL FOOD ·

FRESH HOMEMADE FRUIT SMOOTHIES

Calories

90\245 PEACH MY ASS
00\200 BERRY BERRY BONSAI
50\230 STRAWBERRY SUMMER
90\145 MAD MANGO

Large 4.95
Small 2.50

Fresh Energy Smoothies

90\245 NUTTY IRISHMAN
00\150 Vitamin C booster

Large 5.50 Small 2.80

470 Bangin Blueberry   Large only 6.00
570 Protein Punch   Large only
430 Ladies and Gents   Large only

Organic Wheatgrass Shot 3.30

· Special Nutri Juices ·

ovin dublin
op 10 healthiest
afes\delis dublin

260\130 Fatigue Fighter
180\90 Liver Cleanse

rish times
Best Shops Ireland 2014 150/75 Kick Start
Top 10

· FUEL FOOD ·

FRESH HOMEMADE DETOX

calories

350 Super detox smoothie
350 Fast and Fabulous
350 Brucie Baby
350 Focussed and Fuelled

200 Super detox juice
290 gingzing
490 tastes gut!
290 Auntie Cancer Queen 6.50
350 Cape Clear 6.50
Nutriblend
220 Shine Shine Shine juice
180 Flu Fighter juice
260 Organic juice

· Sejuiced 180\90 cals

· Beet me up! 200\

Large 5.50 Small 2.80

GING
ZING JUICE

 **SERVES: 1**

SF GF DF NF VG

Ingredients
4 small apples
3 carrots
1 lemon, peeled
1 small finger of fresh root
 ginger
1 teaspoon local or manuka
 honey

This zinger of a juice is very popular with our celebrity clientele because it keeps the vocal chords in shape to support a full day's work. High in vitamin C. Low GL.

Juice the apples, carrots, lemon and ginger, then quickly stir in the honey for few seconds. Pour into a glass and serve.

SHINE
SHINE SHINE JUICE

 SERVES: 1

SF GF DF NF V

Ingredients
80g kale
180g fresh spinach
1 medium cucumber
1 hard pear
½ lime, peeled
1 small finger of fresh root ginger

Kale and pear are delicious together in this juice as they complement each other nicely. Just make sure the pear is hard to the touch so it juices well. If it's too ripe, it will just end up in the juice bin. High in calcium. Low GL.

Juice all the ingredients in the order listed. Pour into a glass and serve.

COCO
LOCO SMOOTHIE

 SERVES: 1

Ingredients
2 medium oranges, peeled
250ml coconut milk or
 coconut water
1 banana, peeled
⅕ pineapple, peeled
1 level tablespoon chia seeds
1 level teaspoon coconut oil
A pinch of ground cardamom

If you're feeling down and out, this will get you back to feeling normal again in super quick time because the chia seeds contain essential fats for the brain. These fats create the happy hormone, serotonin, which will make you feel so much better. Plus all these tropical flavours will make you feel like you're on holiday. High in essential fats, dietary fibre and bromelain.

Juice the oranges and add to a blender with the coconut milk, banana, pineapple, chia seeds, coconut oil and ground cardamom. Blend for 15 seconds and pour into a glass.

PROTEIN
PUNCH ENERGY SMOOTHIE

 SERVES: 1

Ingredients
400ml unsweetened almond milk
7 strawberries, topped and tailed
1½ bananas, peeled
¼ mango, peeled and stoned
1 heaped tablespoon hemp or
 pea protein
1 teaspoon golden flaxseed
½ teaspoon spirulina powder

We are increasingly aware of the importance of lowering the amount of cholesterol and saturated fat in our diets. Spirulina, hemp or pea proteins are natural high-protein foods that contain all eight essential amino acids. Amino acids are the building blocks of the protein the body requires, but with none of the cholesterol or saturated fats. This smoothie is a tasty, easy add-in for vegetarians and vegans looking for more complete plant proteins. High in plant protein, essential fats, dietary fibre, magnesium and antioxidants.

Add all the ingredients to a blender and blend for 20 seconds. Pour into a glass and serve immediately.

FAST
AND FABULOUS GREEN SMOOTHIE

🍴 **SERVES: 1**

Ingredients

3 sticks of celery

2 small apples

1 cucumber, peeled

Handful of fresh spinach

½ lime, peeled

½ avocado, peeled and stoned

2 tablespoons fresh
 pineapple, peeled and diced

A pinch of spirulina

This smoothie is very special to me, as it gave me the opportunity to work with my pal Peter Gaynor of Capital Foods at The Restaurant in Brown Thomas, Dublin. It became very popular with clients and customers, so it's a treat to have it loved so much. High in vitamin C, essential fats, dietary fibre, plant protein, bromelain and magnesium. Low GL.

Juice the celery, apples, cucumber, spinach and lime. Add the juice to a blender with the avocado, pineapple and spirulina. Blend for 20 seconds and pour into a glass, bottle or flask.

Keep refrigerated for up to three days and shake well before use.

BEET
ME UP SMOOTHIE

🍴 **SERVES: 1**

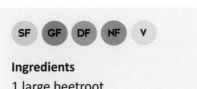

Ingredients

1 large beetroot

2 medium apples

1 small finger of fresh root ginger

2 medium oranges, peeled

1 avocado, peeled and stoned

This smoothie came about from a request from a customer, Peter Foley, and his lovely mum. I added a few extra ingredients and blended it up. It was such a hit, with such a terrific colour and taste, that I had to put it in the book to impress you. High in folic acid, vitamin C and essential fats. Low GL.

Juice the beetroot, apples, ginger and orange, in that order. Add the juice to a blender with the avocado and blend for 10 seconds. Pour into a glass and serve.

ULTIMATE
BREAKFAST SMOOTHIE

🍴 **SERVES: 1**

Ingredients
400ml unsweetened almond milk
¼ small apple, chopped
¼ banana, chopped
2 tablespoons berries
  (blueberries, strawberries or
  raspberries)
1 tablespoon oat flakes
1 tablespoon seeds (sunflower,
  pumpkin or golden flaxseeds)
1 teaspoon manuka honey

This is a smoothie for busy days when you're on the run. Just prep everything the night before to throw into your blender in the morning. High in B vitamins, dietary fibre, essential fats, plant protein, zinc and magnesium.

Pop all the ingredients into a blender and blend for 20 seconds. Easy!

GET UP
AND GO SMOOTHIE

🍴 **SERVES: 1**

Ingredients
4 small apples
1 medium cucumber
1 lime, peeled
⅓ pineapple, peeled and cubed
1 medium avocado, peeled and
  stoned

This is another handy green smoothie if you're stressed out and working hell for leather. Just prepare the ingredients the night before and put it together in the morning. The lime juice is a terrific all-natural preservative, so this will keep in an airtight container in the refrigerator for up to three days. Just shake well before use. High in essential fats, dietary fibre, vitamin C and bromelain. Low GL.

Juice the apples, cucumber and lime. Add the juice to a blender with the avocado and pineapple and blend for 10 seconds. Pour into a glass and serve.

THE LADIES'

SMOOTHIE

🍴 **SERVES: 1**

Ingredients

6 small apples

10g curly parsley

30g alfalfa sprouts

1 banana, peeled

¼ mango, peeled and stoned

1 tablespoon light or dark tahini

1 teaspoon local or manuka
 honey

Two of the main nutrients in this smoothie are calcium and magnesium: calcium in the form of the sesame seeds in the tahini and magnesium in the parsley. Both are vital for bone health and the fight against female osteoporosis, hence the name of this smoothie – but fellas can try it too, of course. It's all about equality! High in dietary fibre, calcium and magnesium. Low GL.

Juice the apples and parsley, then add to a blender with the alfalfa, banana, mango, tahini and honey. Blend for 15 seconds, then pour into a large glass and serve.

BRUCIE

BABY SMOOTHIE

🍴 **SERVES: 1**

Ingredients

6 carrots

1 small finger of fresh root ginger

1 medium avocado, peeled and
 stoned

⅛ pineapple, peeled and chopped

Pinch of ground turmeric

I had to put this recipe in the book as it was given to me by my handsome, happy friend Bruce. He actually got it from his granny in New Zealand and now I would like to pass it on to you. It's delicious and looks amazing. High in essential fats, dietary fibre and bromelain. Low GL.

Juice the carrots and ginger. Add the juice to a blender with the avocado, pineapple and turmeric. Blend for 10 seconds, until smooth. Pour into a glass and serve.

BREAKFAST

When I was young, my mum, God rest her soul, always made sure I had breakfast before I left the house to go to school. Porridge in the winter, boiled eggs and soldiers in the summer, and the odd fry-up if we were good as gold at the weekends. Happy days!

Breakfast is the most important meal of the day and needs to be wholesome and filling. Skipping breakfast rarely helps with weight loss, while just having a coffee or a sugary pastry can lead to weight problems and irritability. Refined sugar and caffeine may make you feel better temporarily, but your body soon 'crashes' from the high, leaving you exhausted or irritable. They also deplete vital nutrients from your system. The sudden raised levels of blood sugar you get from eating refined carbohydrates leads to sudden slumps, which may then cause fatigue and poor concentration.

Breakfast sets you up for the entire day, so put some time into preparing and eating it in a relaxed way, rather than rushing out the door. You will enjoy the experience more this way and breakfast will become a regular meal. The ideal breakfast should have lots of fibre and whole grains, some protein and healthy fat, and as little added sugar as possible – in other words, a good balance of healthy carbohydrates, protein and essential fats.

A nutritious breakfast is important for everyone, no matter what their age, but it is especially critical for children and teenagers. The first two decades of life are ones of remarkable growth and change, and proper nutrition is essential to fuel this transformation from child to adult. Eating breakfast means you are more likely to get your recommended daily intake of vitamins and minerals. It not only contributes to physical health, but also positively affects cognitive function and academic performance, and supports emotional stability and mental alertness. Breakfast also helps promote regular meal patterns and consistent energy intake.

Despite this, breakfast is the most frequently skipped meal – usually because people say they're too busy in the morning or they're just not hungry. A simple remedy is to have something quick and light but satisfying. If you just can't face food first thing in the morning, try easing into it. Sip on a homemade green smoothie throughout the morning or have your oat porridge, natural yoghurt or egg first, then eat your fruit an hour or so later. You'll feel better for it!

SUGAR-FREE
CHIA GRANOLA

 SERVES: 4

Ingredients
160ml maple syrup
2 tablespoons coconut oil,
  melted
1½ tablespoons ground
  cinnamon
⅛ teaspoon Himalayan fine rock
  salt
250g brown rice flakes
125g quinoa flakes
65g pumpkin seeds
65g chia seeds
65g hemp seeds
60g dried cranberries
50g walnuts, chopped
30g dried goji berries
4 dried figs, chopped

I love making this when I have friends staying over. I serve it with chopped ripe banana, natural yoghurt and some honey. High in plant protein, essential fats, dietary fibre, zinc and vitamin E, which is particularly good for the skin. Low GL.

Preheat the oven to 170°C/gas mark 3/325°F.

Combine the maple syrup, melted coconut oil, cinnamon and salt in a small bowl.

Mix the brown rice flakes, quinoa flakes and all the seeds in a large bowl. Pour the liquid mixture into the bowl and mix until uniform (you can use your hands, but make sure they're clean).

Spread the granola on a baking sheet and bake for 45 minutes, until golden. Remove and allow to cool before mixing in the remaining ingredients.

Granola should be kept in an airtight container in the fridge for up to ten days.

EASY BUCKWHEAT
PANCAKES

🍴 **SERVES: 6**

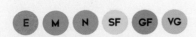

Ingredients
200g buckwheat flour
60ml hot water
60ml dairy cream or almond milk
1 egg, lightly beaten
1½ teaspoons honey
1 teaspoon extra virgin olive oil
Pinch of Himalayan fine rock salt
3 tablespoons coconut oil

Buckwheat contains no gluten and is good for those who need to avoid wheat. These dense, filling and nutritious pancakes are high in protein and fibre and are both tasty and satisfying. High in protein, essential fats and dietary fibre. Low GL.

Place the flour in a large bowl. Add the hot water, cream or almond milk, egg, honey, olive oil and a pinch of salt and mix thoroughly.

Heat the coconut oil in a large frying pan or on a griddle over a medium heat. Pour a ladleful of batter onto the pan and cook both sides until golden brown.

COCONUT
PROTEIN PANCAKES

🍴 **SERVES: 4**

Ingredients
60g mashed banana
3 egg whites
2 tablespoons coconut flour
1 teaspoon unrefined stevia
1 tablespoon coconut oil

Adding berries to the mix or on top is mighty tasty. High in selenium, essential fats, protein and dietary fibre. Low GL.

Mix the mashed banana, egg whites, coconut flour and stevia together using a blender, hand-held blender or wooden spoon until well combined.

Heat the coconut oil in a large frying pan. Pour in a ladleful of batter and cook over a medium heat until the bottom of the pancake is golden brown. Flip over and cook the other side until it's golden brown too.

THE IMPORTANCE OF EGGS

Eggs contain important brain fats called phospholipids. Phospholipids enhance your mood, mind and mental performance. There's no evidence that eating eggs promotes high blood-cholesterol levels or increases the risk of heart disease.

Personally, I like boiling, poaching or scrambling eggs, or making an omelette. When making an omelette, I prefer to use extra virgin olive oil over a low to medium heat for better flavour and texture.

Eggs can help to build muscle and they are rich in protein, cholesterol and vitamins A, B and E. They also contain vitamin D, but only in their yolks, so eat the whole egg to get the whole nutritional package. Organic and free-range chickens spend more time outdoors than any other chickens on the market, and this sun exposure boosts the vitamin D content of their eggs, making them the best choice for both nutrition and sustainability.

EGGCADO

WITH AVOCADO AND CHIVES

 SERVES: 1

Ingredients

2 eggs

1 teaspoon extra virgin olive oil

Himalayan fine rock salt and
  pepper

1 medium, ripe avocado, peeled
  and stoned

1 slice of spelt bread

Pinch of minced fresh chives

This is derived from a recipe my mum made us on Sunday mornings. It's our customers' favourite breakfast at Select Stores, especially Mary Kingston, who gave it the name Eggcado. It's tasty, filling and light. High in protein, dietary fibre and essential fats. Low GL.

Bring plenty of water to boil in a medium saucepan. Put the eggs into the hot water, reduce the heat to a simmer and cook for about 8 minutes, until they are hard-boiled. Place the boiled eggs in a sieve and rinse under cold running water, then peel the eggs quickly.

Mash the peeled, boiled egg with the olive oil and some salt and pepper in a small bowl. Add the avocado and mash until it's quite smooth but still has a slightly chunky texture.

Toast the spelt bread and slice into soldiers. Serve the mashed egg in a small cup and sprinkle the chopped chives on top. Set the cup on a plate and serve the toast soldiers alongside.

POACHED EGGS
WITH MASHED AVOCADO AND WHOLEGRAIN SPELT TOAST

SERVES: 1

Ingredients

235ml water

1 teaspoon white wine vinegar

2 eggs

2 slices of wholegrain spelt bread

1 ripe avocado

Himalayan fine rock salt and
  pepper

This is our simple Sunday morning breakfast at home, perfect with the papers and a glass of freshly squeezed orange juice or a good cup of coffee before we set out on a long walk around the hills. High in protein, essential fats and dietary fibre. Low GL.

Pour the water and vinegar into a small frying pan and bring to a boil. Once the water is bubbling, reduce to a simmer and carefully crack the eggs into the pan, one by one. Cook for 5 minutes, gently pouring the hot water from the pan over the eggs with a spoon until all the egg white is cooked through.

While the eggs are cooking, toast the wholegrain spelt bread. Remove the stone and skin from the avocado and thinly slice the flesh into segments.

Put the slices of toast on a hot plate. Thinly layer each slice with the avocado segments, followed by a poached egg on each. Season with salt and pepper and serve straight away.

VEGETARIAN
OMELETTE

 SERVES: 1

Ingredients
2 eggs
1 tablespoon oat milk
Pinch of Himalayan fine rock salt
Pinch of ground black pepper
Pinch of smoked paprika
1 tablespoon extra virgin olive
 oil
50g chopped mushrooms
50g baby spinach
30g chopped red pepper
30g chopped red onion
Toast, to serve
Chopped ripe avocado, to serve

This is ideal to make the morning after a night out on the town to relieve a hangover. This recipe is full of B vitamins and protein to revitalise the brain. Low GL.

Preheat the oven to 180°C/gas mark 4/325°F.

Beat the eggs with the oat milk, seasoning and paprika in a small bowl with a fork until combined.

Heat the olive oil in an ovenproof frying pan over a low to medium heat, making sure you cover most of the pan with the oil to avoid sticking. Add the mushrooms, baby spinach, red pepper and red onion and sauté for 3 minutes, then add the beaten eggs. Make sure you cover all of the toppings and the base of the pan. Cook for 2–3 minutes.

Put the pan in the oven for 5 minutes, until the eggs are cooked through. Use a cloth or oven gloves to remove the pan, as the handle will be extremely hot. Remove the omelette with a spatula, carefully dislodging the omelette from around the side of the pan first. The omelette should slip right out onto a large plate. You can serve it flat or fold it into a half-moon shape.

Serve with your favourite bread for toast and some chopped ripe avocado.

THE IMPORTANCE OF OATS

Oats are an economical, versatile and nutritious food. They stabilise blood-sugar levels and prevent sugar crashes, as they are full of slow-releasing carbohydrates to give you plenty of energy until lunchtime. They contain a lot of soluble fibre that is rich in beta-glucans. This particular type of fibre has been shown to lower bad cholesterol levels and help prevent high blood pressure. Oats are also rich in the minerals calcium and magnesium, which, as well as strengthening bones, are very important for nerve function, and contain a reasonable amount of B vitamins. B vitamins are very good for your nerves and emotional well-being.

Oats improve circulation and prevent inflammation through an abundance of antioxidants. They boost the immune system to eliminate bad bacteria and fight disease. Oats are also a good source of selenium, manganese and zinc – three minerals that support your body's antioxidant and immune defences. These minerals also help absorb and process omega-3 fats in the body properly.

FRESH BIRCHER
MUESLI WITH MIXED BERRIES AND FLAXSEED

 SERVES: 5

Ingredients
450g oat flakes (use brown
 rice, quinoa or millet flakes if
 you prefer gluten-free grains)
600ml freshly juiced apple
 juice
2 teaspoons ground cinnamon
260g grated pear
260g grated apple
260g natural yoghurt
Juice of 1½ lemons
300g mixed berries
 (strawberries, raspberries and
 blueberries)
3 tablespoons honey
6 tablespoons ground flaxseed

This recipe is a perfect example of food combining: in this meal you get essential fats from the flaxseed, complex carbohydrates and fibre from the oat flakes and protein from the natural yoghurt. This provides fuel for your body to give you more energy over a longer period of time until your next meal.

This Bircher muesli was inspired by North Bondi in Australia and Carmel Somers of the Good Things Café in Durrus, West Cork. I love to make this all the time, as it works not only as a breakfast but also as a snack or dessert. It's another favourite at the shop, particularly in spring and summer, as it's served chilled. High in protein, dietary fibre, essential fats and vitamin C. Low GL.

Place the oat flakes in a large bowl or airtight container. Mix in the apple juice and cinnamon. Add the grated pear, apple, yoghurt and lemon juice and mix well, until all the oats are saturated and there is no dryness left. Cover the bowl with cling film or seal the airtight container. Soak overnight in the refrigerator.

The next morning, spoon into serving bowls. Top with mixed berries, drizzle with honey and add a scattering of ground flaxseed on top.

This will keep for three days in the refrigerator in an airtight container.

VERY BERRY

PORRIDGE

SERVES: 2–3

Ingredients
235ml water
190g jumbo oat flakes
175g fresh strawberries and
 raspberries
2 tablespoons freshly squeezed
 lemon juice
1 tablespoon date syrup
1 teaspoon vanilla extract
1 teaspoon ground cinnamon
1 teaspoon ground turmeric
120g natural yoghurt
2 tablespoons flaked almonds

If you prefer a warmer version of Bircher muesli in the cold autumn and winter months, this is the recipe for you to keep you warm and content before heading out into the elements. High in iron, dietary fibre, plant protein, essential fats and vitamin C. Low GL.

Bring the water to a boil in a saucepan, then reduce to a simmer and add the oats. Cook for about 5 minutes, stirring occasionally.

While the oat flakes are cooking, put the berries in a bowl with the lemon juice, date syrup, vanilla extract, cinnamon and turmeric.

Once the oat flakes are cooked and fluffy, pour them into a large bowl and fold in the yoghurt. Layer on the berry mixture and top with the flaked almonds. Serve immediately.

PORRIDGE
WITH BANANAS

 SERVES: 2

Ingredients

120ml water

70g jumbo oat flakes

65g natural yoghurt

2 teaspoons honey

1 tablespoon flaxseed oil

Pinch of ground cinnamon

2 medium bananas

1 tablespoon freshly squeezed
 lemon juice

1 tablespoon pumpkin seeds

1 tablespoon sunflower seeds

This is a great recipe for kids on dark, cold mornings to get them set up for the day ahead. High in B vitamins, protein and dietary fibre. Low GL.

Bring the water to a boil in a saucepan, then add the oats and reduce to a simmer. Cook for 5–7 minutes, until the oats are a smooth consistency. Add more water if you want the porridge to be thinner. Remove from the heat and stir in the yoghurt, honey, flaxseed oil and cinnamon.

Mash the bananas in a bowl and pour the lemon juice on top, then combine with the oat mixture. Transfer to two serving bowls, sprinkle with the seeds and serve.

SUPER
OAT PANCAKES

 SERVES: 3

Ingredients
270g oat flakes

235ml warm water

115ml natural yoghurt

3 eggs, lightly beaten

2 tablespoons honey or maple
 syrup

1 teaspoon baking powder

1 teaspoon ground cinnamon

1 teaspoon vanilla extract

A pinch of Himalayan fine rock
 salt

Coconut oil or unsalted butter,
 for cooking

Oats contain vitamins, minerals and fibre, which are all vital to our well-being. However, oats also have enzyme inhibitors and other natural substances that can interfere with digestion and block the absorption of all of those great minerals and vitamins. Soaking oats before eating them neutralises the phytates and enzyme inhibitors. In effect, it pre-digests the grains so that all their nutrients are more available. High in dietary fibre and protein. Low GL.

Begin by soaking the oats the night before you plan to make the pancakes. In a medium bowl, mix the oats, warm water and yoghurt until the oats are completely wet. Cover and leave at room temperature for at least 12 hours.

When you're ready to cook the pancakes, combine the soaked oats with the beaten eggs, honey or syrup, baking powder, cinnamon, vanilla extract and salt.

Melt the butter or oil in a frying pan over a medium to high heat. For each pancake, spoon one quarter cup of the batter into the pan and spread until it's 1cm thick. Cook until each side is golden brown.

Serve with a squeeze of lemon, natural yoghurt and mixed berries.

BREADS

I find making bread a very therapeutic thing to do. It's a bit like stroking a cat. Apparently the stroking takes away negative ions and stresses, leaving you refreshed and replenished. I usually make a batch of bread after having a bad day.

SIMPLE WHOLEGRAIN
SPELT BREAD WITH FLAXSEED

 MAKES: 1 SMALL LOAF

Ingredients

225g mixed whole grains (oats,
 wheat grain, barley, etc.)
30g flaxseed
65g white spelt flour
65g wholewheat spelt flour
2 teaspoons baking powder
1 teaspoon Himalayan fine rock
 salt
250ml oat milk
2 tablespoons honey
1 tablespoon extra virgin olive oil

Spelt is an excellent source of complex carbohydrates, plant protein and dietary fibre. It's also high in B vitamins and minerals. Spelt is easy to digest and is a particularly good choice to eat before going on long walks, hikes, cycles or taking part in any other sports event.

Preheat the oven to 230°C/gas mark 8/450°F. Line a baking sheet with parchment paper.

Place the grains and flaxseed in a blender or food processor and pulse to coarsely grind.

Combine the ground grains, flours, baking powder and salt in a large mixing bowl. In a separate bowl, combine the oat milk, honey and olive oil. Pour the liquids into the dry ingredients and stir just until you achieve a soft dough.

Tip the dough out onto a lightly floured surface and gently knead into a round loaf about 8cm round. Place on the lined baking sheet. Place in the oven and immediately reduce the temperature to 220°C/gas mark 7/425°F. Bake for 15–20 minutes, until the crust is a deep golden brown.

This bread is at its best served warm out of the oven.

FUEL FOOD
BANANA AND COCONUT SPELT BREAD

 SERVES: 16

Ingredients

750g mashed ripe bananas
 (about 5 medium bananas)
60ml oat milk
8 tablespoons maple syrup
6 tablespoons coconut oil, plus
 1 tablespoon for greasing the tin
1 teaspoon vanilla extract
130g white spelt flour
130g wholegrain spelt flour
1 teaspoon baking soda
1 teaspoon baking powder
½ teaspoon Himalayan fine rock
 salt
140g chopped walnuts

This is such an easy recipe for banana bread. I love using good-quality maple syrup to give this bread a richer taste and aroma. Maple syrup is very high in the mineral manganese, which contributes greatly to energy production and helps build up the best antioxidant defences against disease.

Preheat the oven to 190°C/gas mark 5/375°F. Grease a 20cm square baking dish with a tablespoon of coconut oil, then dust lightly with some white spelt flour and shake out the excess.

Blend the mashed bananas, oat milk, maple syrup, coconut oil and vanilla extract in a blender until smooth.

In a large bowl, whisk the flours, baking soda, baking powder and salt until well combined. Add the banana mixture and stir to combine, using as few strokes as possible to avoid over-mixing. Fold in the walnuts.

Scrape into the prepared baking dish and smooth the top. Bake for 30–35 minutes, until a toothpick inserted into the centre of the bread comes out clean.

Run a knife around the inside of the baking dish as soon as the bread comes out of the oven, then gently shake the dish from side to side and also in a circular movement to free the bottom. Lay a wire cooling rack on top of the baking dish and turn the dish upside down, making sure you are holding the cooling rack as well. Gently raise the baking dish, freeing the bread from the pan. This will prevent the bread from overcooking and drying out while sitting in the hot baking dish and it will also speed up the cooling time.

Serve with your favourite fruit jam or nut butter, or if served on its own, this is ideal for lunchboxes.

BRUNCH

These are a few of our favourite weekend brunch dishes. Each recipe contains everything you need for a healthy brunch, so you can shine as the morning-after chef when you have friends or family over.

COURGETTE
AND BLUE CHEESE PANCAKES

🍴 **SERVES: 4**

Ingredients

450g grated and drained
  courgettes

Himalayan fine rock salt

150g canned sweetcorn, rinsed
  and drained

145g buckwheat flour

75g shallots, finely chopped

75g blue cheese, crumbled

4 eggs, beaten

1 teaspoon fresh mint, finely
  chopped

1 teaspoon freshly ground black
  pepper

Rapeseed oil for baking/frying

100g rocket leaves, to serve

Courgettes have a high water content during the summer months and are fantastic for hydrating the body. They're also full of carotene, which can protect our skin from the sun. High in dietary fibre, protein, essential fats, antioxidants, vitamin C and selenium. Low GL.

Preheat the oven to 170°C/gas mark 3/325°F.

Toss the grated courgettes with a teaspoon of salt in a colander and spread the mixture evenly on a lightly oiled baking tray. Bake in the oven on the bottom shelf, stirring a few times, for 1 hour or until the courgettes reduce slightly in volume but are still moist. Remove from the oven and allow to cool completely.

In a medium bowl, mix together the cooled courgettes, sweetcorn, buckwheat flour, shallots, blue cheese, eggs, mint and seasonings to form a batter.

Heat a little oil in a large frying pan over a medium heat. When it's hot, add a small ladleful of the batter. Fry the pancakes for about 3 minutes on each side, until golden brown.

Serve immediately, topped with rocket leaves and a pinch of salt and pepper.

HERBY
SMOKED SALMON FRITTATA

 SERVES: 4

Ingredients
3 tablespoons rapeseed oil

2 spring onions, thinly sliced

325g cooked new potatoes, chopped

200g smoked salmon, sliced

3 sun-dried tomatoes, finely chopped

¼ teaspoon chilli flakes

7 eggs

8 fresh basil leaves, torn into small pieces

4 sprigs of fresh tarragon, finely chopped

Himalayan fine rock salt and freshly ground black pepper

When selecting tarragon for this frittata, look for sprigs with a firm stem and lovely straight leaves that aren't wilted or blackened. You can preserve fresh tarragon in vinegar in a glass jar and store it in the refrigerator for up to six months. High in essential fats, protein and dietary fibre. Low GL.

Heat 1 tablespoon of the oil in an ovenproof frying pan or wok over a medium heat. Sauté the spring onions for about 3 minutes, until very soft and lightly browned. Stir in the cooked new potatoes, then turn down the heat and continue cooking for about 5 minutes. Stir in the smoked salmon, sun-dried tomatoes and chilli flakes and cook for 2 minutes, stirring.

While the spring onions are cooking, break the eggs into a bowl and whisk until well blended. Add the herbs and salt and pepper to taste and mix thoroughly.

Preheat the grill to a medium to high heat. Adjust the oven shelf so that it is 13–15cm from the heat.

When the spring onion mixture is cooked, remove it from the pan and let it cool slightly, then mix it into the eggs.

In the frying pan, heat the remaining 2 tablespoons of oil over a medium heat. Add the egg and onion mixture and evenly distribute the ingredients in the pan with a fork. Turn the heat down to medium to low and cook for about 8 minutes. The key is to cook the eggs nice and slowly. If you're not sure, gently slip a spatula under the eggs to see how firm they have become before you set the pan under the grill. When all but the centre of the eggs is done, place the pan under the grill for 30–60 seconds, until the frittata is lightly browned and firm.

Let the finished eggs rest for 10 minutes before serving. Remove the frittata with a spatula, carefully dislodging it from around the sides of the pan first. The frittata should slip right out onto a large plate.

WEST CORK
CHORIZO AND CHEESE OMELETTE

SERVES: 1

Ingredients

2 large eggs

1 tablespoon oat milk

Pinch of smoked paprika

Pinch of Himalayan fine rock salt

Pinch of freshly ground black
  pepper

1 tablespoon extra virgin olive oil

6 slices of chorizo, cut into small
  cubes

4 button mushrooms, chopped

60g red onion, chopped

60g baby spinach

50g Gubbeen or Cheddar cheese,
  grated

Your favourite toasted bread, to
  serve

Salad, to serve

Chopped, ripe avocado, to serve

I particularly like using the chorizo from Gubbeen Farmhouse in West Cork, as I know the Ferguson family who run the farm and the pigs are raised ethically. You can buy this chorizo in any good gourmet shop. Wait until you smell it – your neighbours will be knocking on your door to join you. High in protein and essential fats. Low GL.

Preheat the oven to 180°C/gas mark 4/350°F.

Beat the eggs with the oat milk, smoked paprika and seasoning in a small bowl with a fork until combined.

Heat the olive oil in an ovenproof frying pan over a low to medium heat, making sure you cover most of the pan with the oil to avoid sticking. Add the chorizo, mushrooms, red onion and baby spinach and sauté for 3 minutes, stirring with a wooden spoon.

Add the beaten eggs, making sure you cover all the toppings and the base of the pan. Cook for 2–3 minutes on a medium heat, then add the grated cheese. Put the pan in the oven for 5 minutes, until the eggs are cooked through. Use a cloth or oven gloves to remove the pan, as the handle will be extremely hot.

Remove the omelette with a spatula, carefully dislodging it from around the sides of the pan first. The omelette should slip right out onto a large plate. Serve it flat or fold it into a half-moon shape.

Serve with your favourite bread for toast, or salad and some chopped, ripe avocado.

SMOKED
SALMON OMELETTE

🍴 **SERVES: 1**

Ingredients

2 large eggs

1 tablespoon oat milk

Pinch of Himalayan fine rock salt

Pinch of freshly ground black
 pepper

1 tablespoon extra virgin olive oil

75g smoked salmon, shredded

60g baby spinach

5 cherry tomatoes, chopped

1 spring onion, chopped

Pinch of freshly minced chives

Your favourite toasted bread, to
 serve

Salad, to serve

Chopped, ripe avocado, to serve

This brunch dish is ideal if you prefer something light but filling, especially if you're heading to the gym or going for a nice long walk. High in essential fats and protein. Low GL.

Preheat the oven to 180°C/gas mark 4/350°F.

Beat the eggs with the oat milk and seasoning in a small bowl with a fork until combined.

Heat the olive oil in an ovenproof frying pan over a low to medium heat, making sure you cover most of the pan with the oil to avoid sticking. Add the smoked salmon, baby spinach, cherry tomatoes, spring onion and chives and sauté for 3 minutes, stirring with a wooden spoon.

Add the beaten eggs, making sure you cover all the toppings and the base of the pan. Cook for 2–3 minutes on a medium heat, then put the pan in the oven for 5 minutes, until the eggs are cooked through. Use a cloth or oven gloves to remove the pan, as the handle will be extremely hot.

Remove the omelette with a spatula, carefully dislodging it from around the sides of the pan first. The omelette should slip right out onto a large plate. Serve it flat or fold it into a half-moon shape.

Serve with your favourite toasted bread, or salad and some chopped, ripe avocado.

ULTIMATE

FALAFEL WRAPS WITH MEDITERRANEAN ROAST VEGGIES AND CORIANDER HUMMUS

 MAKES: 6

For the falafel

1 x 400g can of chickpeas • 50g red onion, finely chopped •
25g fresh flat-leaf parsley • 20g fresh coriander • 50ml water •
1 tablespoon freshly squeezed lemon juice • 2 teaspoons ground cumin •
1 teaspoon ground turmeric • 1 teaspoon Himalayan fine rock salt •
100g wholemeal spelt flour • Rapeseed oil, for frying

For the roast Mediterranean vegetables

½ small red onion, chopped • ½ medium courgette, quartered and cut into bite-size chunks •
¼ medium red pepper, chopped • ¼ medium yellow pepper, chopped •
3 sun-dried tomatoes, finely chopped • 3 Kalamata olives, stoned and finely chopped •
1 handful of fresh baby spinach • 2 tablespoons balsamic vinegar •
1 tablespoon extra virgin olive oil • ½ teaspoon Himalayan fine rock salt •
⅛ teaspoon freshly ground black pepper

For the coriander hummus

1 x 400g tin of chickpeas, rinsed and drained • 30g fresh coriander, finely chopped •
Juice of ½ lemon • 35ml water • 35ml extra virgin olive oil • 3 tablespoons light tahini •
¼ teaspoon Himalayan fine rock salt

Salad leaves, to serve • Tortilla wraps, to serve

Chickpeas are a low-fat, high-protein food and work very well with food combining, so you feel fuelled and complete. You should always rinse chickpeas to eliminate any residue from the can or jar. High in dietary fibre and manganese and with a low GL, these are the best wraps in town, perfect for when the match or game is on!

Preheat the oven to 180°C/gas mark 4/350°F.

To make the falafel, rinse the chickpeas and drain them well. Combine all the ingredients except the flour and oil in a food processor and mix until you have a dough. Use a spatula to scrape it into a large bowl, then add the flour and stir until thoroughly combined. Roll between the palms of your clean hands into small balls.

Heat some rapeseed oil in a heavy wok or frying pan over a medium heat. Fry the falafel in batches for 15 minutes, turning often while they're frying so that all the sides are golden. Add a little more oil if needed. Place the cooked falafel on a plate lined with kitchen paper to soak up any excess oil.

To make the roast vegetables, place all the vegetables on a large baking tray or roasting tin and toss with the balsamic vinegar, oil, salt and pepper. Cook for about 20 minutes, until cooked through. Set aside.

To make the hummus, blend all the ingredients in a high-power blender until smooth.

To assemble, start by arranging a selection of your favourite salad leaves on the bottom of each tortilla wrap so that it covers half the tortilla, leaving a small gap at the bottom. Next, arrange the vegetables in a line along the salad leaves. Place three or four falafel on top of the vegetables, then spoon over a generous amount of hummus.

Fold in the left- and right-hand sides of the tortilla, then bring the bottom of the tortilla up over the two sides that have already been folded in. Using your thumbs, and keeping the sides and bottom rolled up, roll the main part of the tortilla towards the top so that it starts to form the wrap and keep everything tightly packed together. Once completely rolled, cut at a diagonal with a sharp knife.

WHOLEFOOD SALADS

To boost your immune system, make sure that you get adequate sleep, keep stress levels low and eat a diet rich in fresh fruits and vegetables. Wholefood salads are key to a happy, healthy immune system.

As an extra savoury topping for any of these salads, I always toast some pumpkin and sunflower seeds on a hot, dry pan with some tamari soya sauce for about 5 minutes on a low heat, until golden, and scatter them over to make the salad complete. This tip was inspired by Pamela and Lorraine Fitzmaurice of Blazing Salads in Dublin, one of our favourite wholefood suppliers for many years.

Pumpkin seeds and sunflower seeds are a good source of zinc and essential fatty acids. They are particularly beneficial for men and the prostate gland. One of the highest concentrations of zinc in the body is found in the prostate gland, so it's important for men to keep their zinc levels topped up.

AVOCADO
AND SWEET POTATO SALAD

SERVES: 4

SOY SF GF DF NF V

Ingredients
3 large sweet potatoes, peeled and diced

2 tablespoons coconut oil, melted

3 medium avocados, peeled, stoned and diced

For an easy dressing
150ml coconut aminos

150ml apple cider vinegar

Extra virgin olive oil, to taste

Himalayan fine rock salt and freshly ground black pepper

For a complex dressing
150ml liquid aminos

150ml apple cider vinegar

60ml extra virgin olive oil

Juice of 1 large orange or 2 lemons/limes

2 tablespoons freshly grated root ginger

1 tablespoon crushed garlic

1 teaspoon chilli flakes

Himalayan fine rock salt and freshly ground black pepper

Avocados are a great introduction to solid foods for babies. Their buttery, creamy texture is easy for babies to chew on and swallow safely. Rich in omega-3s and other nutrients, avocados also offer babies a healthy source of plant-based fat. Be sure to pick an avocado that gives slightly when squeezed but is not mushy. Blend the avocado in a blender with a little water if you want to thin the mixture out.

Avocados also include essential fats and may help to lower cholesterol levels. This recipe is high in vitamin C, fibre, potassium and plant protein, but you could add some grilled chicken or fish if you like your meat.

Preheat the oven to 200°C/gas mark 6/400°F.

Place the sweet potatoes on a large baking tray in a single layer and toss them in the melted coconut oil. Cover the tray with tinfoil and roast in the oven for 30 minutes. Uncover the tray and cook for 10 minutes more, until the potatoes are caramelised a bit and tender all the way through. Let cool.

Meanwhile, whisk your chosen dressing ingredients together in a medium-sized bowl until well combined.

Toss the sweet potatoes with the dressing. Add the diced avocados, mix gently and serve.

BEETROOT,
BUTTERNUT SQUASH AND FETA SALAD

 SERVES: 4

Ingredients
600g butternut squash
1 tablespoon rapeseed oil or
 extra virgin olive oil
Himalayan fine rock salt and
 freshly ground black pepper
2 medium beetroots
200g baby spinach, washed
150g feta cheese, crumbled

For the dressing
3 tablespoons extra virgin olive
 oil
1 tablespoon balsamic vinegar
1 tablespoon orange juice
Himalayan fine rock salt and
 freshly ground black pepper

I add protein rich feta cheese to this tangy salad to add richness in flavour. It's an ideal salad for recovery after a gruelling workout with your friends. High in vitamin C and protein. Although feta is made from sheep's and goat's rather than cow's milk, there is some disagreement as to whether these can trigger a dairy intolerance, so I have erred on the side of caution and listed any recipe containing feta with the 'contains milk' symbol.

Preheat the oven to 200°C/gas mark 6/400°F.

Chop the butternut squash into 5cm cubes (you can leave the skin on if preferred) and place on a baking tray. Drizzle with the oil and sprinkle with salt and pepper. Bake for 25–30 minutes, until tender.

Meanwhile, peel the beetroots and chop them into 5cm cubes. Place in a pan and cover with water. Add a sprinkle of salt and bring to a boil, then reduce the heat to a simmer and cook for about 20 minutes, until tender. Drain.

Place the washed baby spinach in a bowl. Add the warm beetroot and butternut squash, then sprinkle over the feta and gently toss all the ingredients together.

To make the dressing, whisk together the olive oil, balsamic vinegar and orange juice and season to taste with salt and pepper, then drizzle over the salad and serve.

BROCCOLI
AND SESAME SEED SALAD

SERVES: 4

Ingredients
300g broccoli

120g French beans

180g mangetout

1 tablespoon sesame oil

20g fresh coriander leaves

3 tablespoons toasted sesame
 seeds

1 teaspoon nigella seeds

150g baby spinach

For the dressing
50g light tahini

40ml water

1 small clove of garlic, crushed

1½ tablespoons mirin

¾ tablespoon apple cider vinegar

½ tablespoon honey (or less if
 preferred)

½ teaspoon tamari

Pinch of Himalayan fine rock salt

Even though the sesame seed is one of the smallest edible seeds around, it's packed with nutrients, especially calcium. One cup of sesame seeds has a 4:1 ratio of calcium compared to a cup of whole milk. High in fibre, vitamin C, calcium and magnesium.

Whisk together all the dressing ingredients in a small bowl. It should be smooth and thick, so adjust the amount of water if necessary. Season to taste.

Trim off any leaves from the broccoli. If the florets are thick, cut them lengthways into two or four so that you are left with long, thin stalks, similar to the French beans. Top and tail the beans and mangetout, keeping them separate.

Bring a medium-sized pan of unsalted water to a boil. Blanch the French beans for 3–5 minutes, until tender but still crunchy. Lift the beans into a colander with a slotted spoon and refresh under cold running water, then drain and dry well with a tea towel. Using the same water, blanch the mangetout for 2 minutes. Lift into a colander with a slotted spoon and refresh, drain and pat dry. Repeat this process for the broccoli, blanching for 2–3 minutes. Mix all the blanched vegetables together in a large bowl with the sesame oil.

Stir most of the coriander leaves, sesame seeds and nigella seeds in with the vegetables, then mix in the baby spinach. Pile it all onto a serving dish, pour the dressing on top and top with the remaining coriander and seeds.

GOZO

PUY LENTIL SALAD

🍴 **SERVES: 4**

Ingredients
260g Puy lentils
750ml water
180g cherry tomatoes, halved
1 small red onion, chopped
½ cucumber, cut into cubes
1 clove of garlic, minced
20g chopped fresh oregano
2 tablespoons chopped fresh
  flat-leaf parsley
2 tablespoons chopped fresh
  mint
230g feta cheese

For the vinaigrette
6 tablespoons extra virgin olive
  oil
Zest of 2 lemons
90ml freshly squeezed lemon
  juice
Himalayan fine rock salt and
  freshly ground black pepper

This salad is so delicious on its own – the creaminess of the feta against the crunchy cucumber and sweet tomatoes is a perfect combination – and adding lentils is an easy way to up the protein content. This classic salad is just the lunchtime pick-me-up I need to give me the energy to attack the rest of the day. Add grilled salmon, chicken, tofu or prawns for even more of a protein boost if you're extra hungry. High in calcium, vitamin C and fibre.

Place the lentils in a saucepan with the water and bring to a boil. Reduce the heat and simmer for approximately 20 minutes, until the lentils are tender. Drain and set aside in a large bowl.

To make the vinaigrette, whisk together the olive oil, lemon zest and juice, and a generous seasoning of salt and pepper in a small bowl. It should be well seasoned because it will be tossed with the rest of the ingredients.

Add the vinaigrette to the lentils and allow the lentils to fully cool. When cooled, add the tomatoes, red onion, cucumber, garlic and herbs. Stir gently to combine.

Transfer the salad to a large serving platter and crumble the feta over the top.

QUINOA

GREEN BEAN SALAD

🍴 **SERVES: 4**

Ingredients

200g quinoa
500ml water
Himalayan fine rock salt
240g fresh French beans
310g canned chickpeas, rinsed
  and drained
160g canned kidney beans,
  rinsed and drained
100g roasted red peppers from a
  jar, rinsed, drained and chopped
1 teaspoon dried tarragon
Freshly ground black pepper

For the dressing

3 tablespoons extra virgin olive
  oil
1 tablespoon balsamic vinegar

Quinoa (pronounced KEEN-wah) is a light whole grain with plenty of protein. Once you try it, you'll invite it back to your table again and again. Always wash the quinoa in a sieve before you use it to remove any grit or dirt. Use a wooden spoon to gently clean the grain. Taste a grain, and if it's bitter, wash it some more.

You can substitute any of the three beans with what you can get on sale or from your garden. Canned pinto or black beans are fine too. This beautiful, delicious summer salad works as a side dish or as a vegetarian starter. High in protein, magnesium and fibre.

Rinse the quinoa under cold running water and drain. Bring the water to a boil in a small pot. Stir in the quinoa and a pinch of salt. Reduce the heat, cover and simmer for 15–20 minutes, until the quinoa is fluffy and tender and all the water has been absorbed. Remove from the heat, uncover and let it cool.

Meanwhile, bring a medium-sized pan of unsalted water to a boil. Top and tail the French beans and cut them into 5cm pieces. Blanch these beans for 3–5 minutes, until tender but still crunchy. Lift them into a colander with a slotted spoon and refresh under cold running water, then drain and dry well with a tea towel.

Whisk together the olive oil and balsamic vinegar in a small bowl. Put the cooled quinoa in a large bowl with the French beans, chickpeas, kidney beans, red pepper, tarragon and some salt and pepper and toss with the dressing. Serve chilled or at room temperature.

THE PROUD
QUINOA SALAD

SERVES: 4

Ingredients
80g walnuts
180g quinoa
400ml water
Himalayan fine rock salt
3 tablespoons extra virgin olive oil
3 tablespoons freshly squeezed lemon juice
1 tablespoon sherry vinegar
Zest of 1 lemon
2 tablespoons chopped fresh parsley
2 tablespoons chopped fresh basil
2 tablespoons diced red onion
1 clove of garlic, minced
170g red cabbage, finely chopped or shredded
70g feta cheese, crumbled
60g chopped Kalamata olives
1 Granny Smith apple, chopped into small cubes
1 yellow bell pepper, chopped

Make sure you keep your walnuts in an airtight container in a cool, dark place to keep them fresh, as they're very perishable – and that goes for any whole nut or seed. If you leave them out, they will go rancid. This salad is loud and proud, so only use the best nuts for this baby. High in protein and antioxidants.

Preheat the oven to 170°C/gas mark 3/325°F. Spread out the walnuts on a small baking tray and roast for 5–7 minutes. Set aside to cool, then roughly chop.

Rinse the quinoa in a fine-mesh strainer. Put the quinoa in a dry frying pan set over a medium to low heat and toast for 5 minutes, stirring frequently, until aromatic.

Bring the water to a boil in a medium-sized pot. Stir in the toasted quinoa and a pinch of salt. Reduce the heat, cover and simmer for 15–20 minutes, until the quinoa is fluffy and tender and all the water has been absorbed. Remove from the heat and let it cool.

In a large serving bowl, whisk together the oil, lemon juice, sherry vinegar, lemon zest and ½ teaspoon of salt. Stir the fresh herbs, red onion and garlic into the dressing, then fold in the remaining salad ingredients along with the cooled quinoa and the toasted walnuts. Serve at room temperature.

HALLOUMI
AND COURGETTE CORN PASTA SALAD

 SERVES: 4

Ingredients

3 medium courgettes, grated

1½ tablespoons red wine vinegar

100g frozen shelled edamame beans

50g fresh basil leaves, coarsely shredded

15g fresh parsley leaves

75ml olive oil

Himalayan fine rock salt and freshly ground black pepper

250g corn pasta

200g halloumi cheese, thickly sliced

200g rocket

Grated zest of 1 lemon

1½ tablespoons small capers

When I make this salad I shred the fresh basil leaves to release their natural oils, which are fantastic for digestion as they can relax the digestive tract to process and absorb food effectively. High in iron, vitamin C and protein.

Tip the grated courgette into a bowl, pour over the vinegar and stir. Set aside.

Bring a pan of water to a boil. Add the edamame beans and blanch for 3 minutes. Drain and refresh under cold running water, then set aside to dry.

Combine half the basil, all the parsley and the olive oil in a small food processor along with a bit of salt and pepper. Blitz to a smooth sauce and set aside.

Cook the pasta in boiling salted water until al dente or according to the instructions on the packet. Drain the pasta, rinse under cold running water and leave to dry, then return it to the pan in which it was cooked.

Fry the slices of halloumi cheese on a hot, dry frying pan for 3 minutes on each side, until golden. Cut into cubes and set aside.

Pour the courgettes and their vinegary juices over the pasta. Add the edamame beans, basil sauce, rocket, lemon zest, capers and halloumi. Gently stir together, then taste and season with plenty of salt and pepper. Stir in the remaining basil just before serving.

POPEYE

SPINACH AND POTATO SALAD

 SERVES: 4

Ingredients

800g baby new potatoes, washed
  but not scrubbed
150g frozen petit pois
60g pine nuts
20g fresh basil leaves
20g fresh flat-leaf parsley leaves,
  plus extra for garnish
2 cloves of garlic, crushed
1 tablespoon nutritional yeast
200ml extra virgin olive oil
200g baby spinach
½ teaspoon white wine vinegar
2 tablespoons finely shredded
  fresh mint leaves
Himalayan fine rock salt and
  freshly ground black pepper

Spinach has lots of vitamin K and twice as much iron as most greens, restoring energy and increasing vitality – the source of Popeye's strength. High in dietary fibre, essential fats, plant protein, iron, calcium and magnesium. Low GL.

Cook the potatoes in a pan of boiling water for 15–20 minutes, until soft but not falling apart. Drain the potatoes and cut them in half as soon as they are cool enough to handle, but still warm.

Blanch the peas in a separate pan of boiling water for 30 seconds, then drain and refresh under cold running water. Set aside.

While the potatoes are cooking, place the pine nuts, basil, parsley, garlic and nutritional yeast in a food processor and blitz to a paste. Add the oil and pulse until you get a runny pesto, then pour into a large bowl.

Add the warm potatoes to the bowl and toss in the pesto along with the baby spinach, peas, vinegar and mint. Mix well, even crushing the potatoes slightly so that all the flavours mix. Taste and season, then garnish with a little chopped fresh parsley.

SPICY KALE,
CARROT AND EDAMAME BEAN SALAD

 SERVES: 4

Ingredients
250g kale

200g frozen edamame beans

600ml water

1kg carrots, cut into julienne
 strips

Pinch of Himalayan fine rock salt

1 tablespoon extra virgin olive oil

1 medium onion, finely chopped

1 spring onion, finely chopped

40g fresh coriander, chopped

For the dressing
80ml extra virgin olive oil, plus
 extra

3 cloves of garlic, crushed

2 medium fresh green chillies,
 finely chopped

1 tablespoon white wine vinegar

1 tablespoon chopped preserved
 lemon or lemon juice

1 teaspoon sweet paprika

1 teaspoon ground cumin

¾ teaspoon ground cinnamon

½ teaspoon ground coriander

¼ teaspoon ground cloves

¼ teaspoon ground ginger

Carrots are the Specsavers of vegetables. They promote excellent vision, especially at night, because of their high beta-carotene content, which is beneficial for eye function. High in plant protein, dietary fibre, essential fats and vitamin C. Low GL.

Whisk all the ingredients for the dressing together in a bowl and set aside.

Cut the kale leaves away from the stalk. Discard the stalk and shred the leaves. Place the shredded kale and frozen edamame beans in a wok or large saucepan and cover. Cook for 5–8 minutes over a low to medium heat, until tender. Drain and set aside.

Place the water in a large saucepan and bring to a boil, then add the carrots and a pinch of salt. Boil for about 3 minutes, until they are tender but still crunchy. Drain in a colander and leave to dry.

Heat the oil in a large pan over a low heat. Sauté the onion for 12 minutes, until soft and slightly browned. Remove from the heat and transfer to a large salad bowl. Add in the cooked kale, edamame beans, carrots and spring onion. Give it a big stir and leave to cool.

Stir in the coriander and dressing just before serving, or have the dressing on the side.

SELECT STORES

ASIAN MAYO-FREE COLESLAW

SE · N · SOY · SF · GF · DF · V

Ingredients

150g flaked almonds

1 tablespoon coconut oil

½ teaspoon chilli flakes

½ teaspoon Himalayan fine rock salt

½ head of white cabbage, finely shredded

½ head of red cabbage, finely shredded

3 carrots, grated

1 onion, finely chopped

1 fresh red chilli, deseeded and finely sliced

20g fresh coriander, roughly chopped

15g fresh mint leaves, roughly chopped

For the dressing

100ml freshly squeezed lime juice

20g fresh coriander leaves, roughly chopped

1 lemongrass stalk, chopped into small pieces

3 tablespoons maple syrup

1 teaspoon tamari

¼ teaspoon chilli flakes

4 tablespoons extra virgin olive oil

2 tablespoons toasted sesame oil

Cabbage is a locally grown cruciferous vegetable with a huge phytochemical content, making it an exceptional anti-cancer food. Cabbage is cream of the crop! High in dietary fibre, plant protein, essential fats and vitamin C. Low GL.

To make the dressing, place all the ingredients except the olive oil and sesame oil in a small saucepan and reduce over a high heat for 5–10 minutes, until thick and syrupy. Remove from the heat. Once cooled, strain the dressing into a bowl and add the oils. Set aside.

To caramelise the almonds, place them in a hot, dry frying pan and toast for a few minutes, stirring occasionally, until they are lightly golden on both sides. Turn the heat down to medium and add the coconut oil. Once it's melted add the chilli flakes and salt. Use a wooden spoon to stir constantly for 2 minutes to coat the nuts. Turn out onto a sheet of greaseproof paper and allow to cool, then roughly chop.

Place the shredded cabbage in a large mixing bowl with the rest of the coleslaw ingredients, including the nuts. Add the dressing and toss. Taste and season with a little more salt and pepper if necessary.

SNAPPY
BEAN SALAD

🍴 **SERVES: 4**

Ingredients

3 tablespoons apple cider vinegar
 or rice vinegar

3 tablespoons water

1 tablespoon tamari

1 tablespoon light tahini

1 teaspoon Dijon mustard

1 x 400g can of cannellini beans,
 drained and rinsed

60g spring onions, thinly sliced

60g grated carrots

15g fresh flat-leaf parsley,
 chopped

For a delicious lunch, fill pitta bread halves with this tangy bean salad and top with shredded lettuce. High in dietary fibre, plant protein, essential fats and iron. Low GL.

Whisk together the vinegar, water, tamari, tahini and mustard in a medium bowl. Add the cannellini beans, spring onions, carrots and parsley. Toss to combine and set aside at room temperature to let the flavours blend together for at least 15 minutes before serving.

WARM CHICKPEA,
AUBERGINE AND BROCCOLI SALAD

SERVES: 4

SOY SF DF GF NF V

Ingredients

2 medium aubergines, halved
  lengthways and cut into 1cm-thick
  slices
Extra virgin olive oil, for tossing
25g sunflower seeds
2 teaspoons tamari
250ml water
400g broccoli, broken into florets
Himalayan fine rock salt and freshly
  ground black pepper

For the millet

50g millet
125ml hot water
1 x 400g can of chickpeas, rinsed and
  drained
3 tomatoes, deseeded and diced
3 spring onions, sliced thinly at an angle
3 cloves of garlic, sliced
1 fresh red chilli, deseeded and thinly
  sliced
3 tablespoons chopped fresh flat-leaf
  parsley
3 tablespoons chopped fresh coriander,
  plus extra leaves to garnish
2 teaspoons cumin seeds

For the lemon dressing

Juice of 1 lemon
200ml extra virgin olive oil

I recommend tenderising the aubergine with a wooden mallet to reduce the bitterness. Rub it with a little Himalayan fine rock salt and leave for 15 minutes, as the salt will extract some of the water content and the bitterness too. High in plant protein, essential fats, dietary fibre and calcium. Low GL.

Preheat the oven to 200°C/gas mark 6/400°F. Line a baking tray with parchment paper.

Spread out the aubergine slices on the lined tray and toss lightly in a little olive oil. Roast for 10–12 minutes, until well coloured on both sides, turning once if necessary. Set aside.

Toast the sunflower seeds in a dry, heavy frying pan over a low heat for 8–10 minutes, until lightly coloured. Stir in the tamari and remove from the heat. Transfer the seeds to a bowl and leave to cool.

Pour the water into the base of a wok or large saucepan and bring to a boil. Blanch the broccoli for 3 minutes. Drain and rinse immediately under cold running water to maintain the bright colour of the vegetables after cooking. Season with salt and pepper and set aside.

Toast the millet in a small, dry frying pan over a medium heat for 5 minutes, stirring frequently. Add the hot water and stir once, then cover the pan, remove from the heat and leave for 20 minutes. Fluff up the millet with a fork and put it in a large salad bowl or mixing bowl. Add in the remaining millet ingredients, mixing well with the fork, then add the aubergines and broccoli.

Whisk together the lemon juice and olive oil in a small bowl with a fork. Pour the dressing over the salad and mix well. Garnish with the sunflower seeds and coriander leaves.

BEETROOT
AND GOATS' CHEESE SALAD WITH WALNUTS

SERVES: 4

Ingredients
400g tennis ball-sized beetroots

2 tablespoons coconut oil, melted

2 cloves of garlic, crushed (optional)

75g walnuts

300ml water

100g Puy lentils

½ large onion, finely sliced

15g fresh flat-leaf parsley leaves, roughly chopped

150g baby spinach

100g soft goats' cheese, crumbled

For the dressing
2 tablespoons extra virgin olive oil

1½ tablespoons balsamic vinegar

1 tablespoon freshly squeezed lemon juice

½ teaspoon Dijon mustard

Himalayan fine rock salt and freshly ground black pepper

Fibre-rich lentils may help to lower cholesterol, balance blood sugars and even increase your energy. This is one of our favourite salads at Select Stores, loved by customers, friends and family. It's wholesome, flavoursome and 'meaty', even though it's vegetarian. Roasting nuts enhances their flavour, but they are still delightful when raw. All the goodness of walnuts is retained when they are eaten raw, as essential fatty acids may be destroyed with heat. High in vitamin E, folic acid, protein, essential fats, dietary fibre and vitamin C. Low GL.

Preheat the oven to 220°C/gas mark 7/425°F.

Place the beetroot on a baking tray with the melted coconut oil and garlic, if using. Roast for 40–45 minutes, until tender. If the beetroots are large, you can cut them in half to reduce the cooking time. Remove from the oven and cut into small wedges once they're cool enough to handle.

When the beetroot comes out of the oven, reduce the temperature to 150°C/gas mark 2/300°F. Spread out the walnuts on a baking tray and roast for 10–15 minutes, until nicely toasted. Set aside.

Bring the water to a boil in a saucepan. Add in the lentils, then reduce the heat and simmer for 15 minutes, until cooked through. Drain and set aside.

To make the dressing, whisk together the olive oil, balsamic vinegar, lemon juice, mustard and salt and pepper to taste in a small bowl.

Place the beetroot, sliced onion and chopped parsley in the bowl with the lentils. Add half of the dressing and mix through.

Divide the spinach leaves between four salad plates, top with the beetroot and lentil mixture. Crumble over the goats' cheese and sprinkle the walnuts on top, then drizzle over the rest of the dressing and enjoy.

FUEL FOOD

ORZO SALAD

 SERVES: 2

Ingredients
200g orzo
175g broccoli florets
½ small cucumber, peeled
150g canned sweetcorn, rinsed
 and drained
1 medium carrot, finely chopped
1 medium red onion, finely
 chopped
120ml extra virgin olive oil
120ml balsamic vinegar
1 tablespoon freshly squeezed
 lemon juice
1 teaspoon chopped fresh thyme
1 teaspoon chopped fresh
 rosemary
Himalayan fine rock salt and
 freshly ground black pepper

This delicious, hearty and healthy salad is a great dinner or BBQ dish. It has so many wonderful ingredients that there is something to please everybody. It's great for the cook, too, as it can be prepared ahead of time and is ready to serve when hunger hits!

If you like black pepper, it does more than just add flavour to foods. Black pepper can stimulate your pancreas to release digestive enzymes and has been shown to increase the absorption of selenium and B vitamins found in other spices we consume. High in B vitamins, complex carbohydrates, dietary fibre, plant protein and essential fats. Low GL.

Cook the orzo in a large pot of boiling salted water until al dente or according to the packet instructions. Drain well and set aside.

Meanwhile, blanch the broccoli in a separate large pot of boiling salted water for 3 minutes. Drain and rinse immediately under cold running water to maintain the bright colour of the vegetable after cooking.

Cut the cucumber in half lengthwise and scrape out the seeds, then cut into chunks.

Put all the vegetables into a large mixing bowl along with the olive oil, balsamic vinegar, lemon juice and herbs and mix thoroughly. Add the orzo last and mix thoroughly again. (The reason the orzo is added last is so that it doesn't soak up all the dressing.) Season with salt and pepper and serve.

SOUPS

Homemade soups have been a major part of Select Stores over the years. Our mum always had a pot on the stove for family and visitors. I like to think of them as hot vegetable smoothies, as they are a fantastic way to consume veggies over the winter period for lunch or dinner. It's always best to eat warm foods when it's cold outside to keep your body happy.

BUTTERNUT,
COCONUT AND CORIANDER SOUP

𝄪 **SERVES: 8**

C SF GF DF NF V

Ingredients
2 tablespoons extra virgin olive
 oil
2 large onions, chopped
3kg butternut squash, peeled
 and cut into 5cm cubes
3 cloves of garlic, minced
2½ litres gluten-free vegetable
 stock (you can use less or more
 according to desired thickness)
2 teaspoons ground coriander
160g creamed coconut, grated
Juice of 1 lime
Himalayan fine rock salt and
 freshly ground black pepper
Crusty bread, to serve

I love to grate fresh turmeric into this soup to give it a more powerful flavour and colour. Make sure to use choose a gluten-free stock, such as Kallo or Marigold. High in dietary fibre, plant protein, essential fats and vitamin C. Low GL.

Heat the oil in a large saucepan over a low to medium heat. Sauté the onion for 5–7 minutes, until tender. Add the butternut squash and garlic and stir for a further minute or two.

Add the vegetable stock and ground coriander and bring to a boil. Simmer for 20–30 minutes, until the squash is cooked. Stir in the grated creamed coconut and leave to stand for a minute so that it can melt into the soup. Blend until smooth.

Stir in the lime juice and salt and pepper to taste, and serve with crusty bread.

CAULIFLOWER
AND SWEET POTATO SOUP

 SERVES: 8

Ingredients
500g cauliflower florets, cut into
 small pieces
1 tablespoon garam masala
Extra virgin olive oil, for drizzling
500g sweet potato, peeled and
 diced into medium-sized cubes
1 red onion, diced
2 cloves of garlic, minced
1 litre gluten-free vegetable
 stock
700ml water
Himalayan fine rock salt and
 freshly ground black pepper

A warming, tasty, thick and nutrient-rich soup that's perfect for lunch or dinner. High in vitamin C, essential fats, dietary fibre and plant protein.

Preheat the oven to 200°C/gas mark 6/400°F. Line a baking tray with parchment paper.

Place the cauliflower on the lined baking tray, sprinkle with the garam masala and lightly drizzle with olive oil. Place in the oven and roast for 20–30 minutes, until golden brown on top and tender. Remove from the oven and let it cool while you prepare the soup.

Add the sweet potato, red onion, garlic, vegetable stock and water to a large pot and bring to a boil. Add salt to taste, then reduce the heat and simmer for 30 minutes, until the sweet potatoes are tender. Stir in the cooked cauliflower.

Let the soup cool slightly, then blend with a hand-held blender until very smooth. Season with salt and pepper to taste, reheat and serve.

VEGAN

COCONUT LENTIL SOUP

 SERVES: 5

Ingredients

2 tablespoons coconut oil

1 onion, finely chopped

1 shallot, sliced

1 clove of garlic, minced

1 tablespoon red curry paste

200g split red lentils, rinsed and
 drained

200g brown basmati rice

1½ litres water

1 x 400ml can of coconut milk

Juice of 1 lime

75g golden raisins

2 tablespoons agave syrup

2 tablespoons shoyu soya sauce

1 tablespoon ground turmeric

2 teaspoons Himalayan fine rock
 salt

Toasted coconut flakes and
 minced fresh coriander, to
 garnish

The flavour of this creamed soup is dramatically enhanced by the addition of organic coconut milk. Try it in a tomato soup or chowder too. High in plant protein, essential fats and dietary fibre.

Heat the coconut oil in a large stock pot over a medium to high heat. Add the onion and shallot and sauté for 5 minutes, until softened.

Add the garlic and curry paste, stirring until the paste has dissolved and is well mixed, then add the lentils, rice and water. Bring to a boil, then reduce the heat and simmer for 20–30 minutes, until the rice has cooked through.

Stir in the coconut milk, lime juice, raisins, agave syrup, shoyu sauce, turmeric and salt. Simmer for 10 minutes and serve. Garnish with some toasted coconut flakes and minced fresh coriander.

PUY LENTIL

MINESTRONE

 SERVES: 6

Ingredients

2 tablespoons extra virgin olive
  oil
2 small red onions, finely
  chopped
1 leek, washed, halved
  lengthwise and finely sliced
1 fennel bulb, finely chopped
4 cloves of garlic, finely chopped
2 x 400g tins of good-quality
  chopped tomatoes
150g Puy lentils, rinsed
80g brown basmati rice, rinsed
1½ litres good-quality, gluten-
  free vegetable stock
Himalayan fine rock salt and
  freshly ground black pepper
200g spinach, roughly chopped
80g sweetcorn kernels (fresh,
  canned or frozen)
Toasted crusty bread, to serve

Tomatoes are a nutritious addition to autumnal soups. When no one's looking, I throw a handful of minced sun-dried tomatoes into this soup to intensify the body and flavour. It is important to use a good-quality vegetable broth. As when cooking with wine, if you wouldn't drink a glass of it on its own, then don't cook with it. I usually cook with Marigold or Kallo vegetable bouillon cubes as I find they lend the best quality of flavour to soups and stews. Also, use what's in season. Minestrone is a great way to throw in all your favourite vegetables that are currently in abundance. High in plant protein, essential fats, dietary fibre, lycopene, iron and B vitamins. Low GL.

Heat the oil in a large pot over a low to medium heat. Add the onions, leek, fennel and garlic, partially cover with a lid and sauté for 15 minutes. Don't let them brown – just let them sweat with the lid slightly ajar.

Add the tomatoes, lentils, rice and stock. Bring to a boil, then reduce the heat and simmer. At this point you can taste the broth and season with salt and pepper. Continue to simmer over a medium heat for 20–25 minutes, until the lentils and rice are cooked through.

Add the spinach and sweetcorn, stirring for 1–2 minutes until the spinach begins to wilt.

This doubles as a hearty soup or stew. A meal in itself! Serve with your favourite toasted bread.

LEEK
AND CHICKPEA SOUP

 SERVES: 2

Ingredients

30g unsalted butter

8 saffron threads

1 large leek, cleaned and finely
 sliced

1 carrot, coarsely grated

Zest of 1 small lemon

2 tablespoons roughly chopped
 fresh flat-leaf parsley

1 x 400g can of chickpeas,
 drained and rinsed

550ml gluten-free chicken stock

Himalayan fine rock salt and
 freshly ground black pepper

I lived on this soup when I worked in Rome when I was eighteen. I had an amazing greengrocer beside me that had all the ingredients. I made it all the time, as I couldn't speak Italian, so it was easy for everyone, if you know what I mean! I sometimes add orzo pasta or pearl barley to this recipe and the soup tastes even better. **High in dietary fibre and protein. Low GL.**

Heat the butter and saffron threads in a medium saucepan over a medium heat. Add the leek when the butter begins to bubble and cook for 5 minutes, until it's soft and transparent.

Add the carrot, lemon zest and parsley and cook for 1 minute more before adding the chickpeas and stock. Season to taste and bring to a boil, then reduce the heat and simmer for 15 minutes.

PUMPKIN
AND POTATO SOUP

SERVES: 2

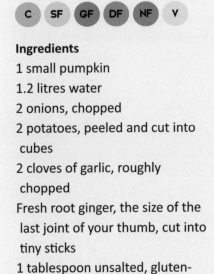

C SF GF DF NF V

Ingredients

1 small pumpkin

1.2 litres water

2 onions, chopped

2 potatoes, peeled and cut into
cubes

2 cloves of garlic, roughly
chopped

Fresh root ginger, the size of the
last joint of your thumb, cut into
tiny sticks

1 tablespoon unsalted, gluten-
free vegetable bouillon

⅛ teaspoon cayenne pepper

Extra virgin olive oil, for drizzling
(optional)

Pinch of minced fresh chives, to
garnish (optional)

Garlic is a valuable addition to this soup, improving the nutritional benefits as well as the flavour. When you chop or mince garlic, you release the unique nutrient allicin, which has major antibacterial properties that can kill germs within the body. High in vitamin C and dietary fibre. Low GL.

Cut the pumpkin in half and scrape out the seeds. Remove the hard outer peel with a vegetable peeler or paring knife and cut the flesh into medium-sized pieces. Boil for 20 minutes in lightly salted water. Drain and set aside.

Heat 1.2 litres of water in a large saucepan. As it comes to a boil, add the pumpkin, onions, potatoes, garlic, ginger, bouillon and cayenne. Reduce the heat to a simmer, cover and cook for 30 minutes, until the potatoes are cooked through.

Roughly purée with a hand-held blender – you want to keep some texture – and serve. You can top each bowl of soup with a little extra virgin olive oil and a pinch of minced chives if you wish.

FUEL FOOD

ROAST TOMATO SOUP

 SERVES: 4

Ingredients

16 medium-sized ripe tomatoes

Himalayan fine rock salt

Cracked black pepper

8 cloves of garlic, peeled

1 tablespoon rapeseed oil

200g quinoa

400ml water

1½ teaspoons ground coriander

1½ teaspoons paprika

1 teaspoon ground cumin

750ml gluten-free vegetable
stock

2 tablespoons crumbled feta
cheese

2 tablespoons minced fresh
chives or finely chopped spring
onions

In this recipe we add high-in-plant-protein quinoa, but
you can use millet or short-grain brown rice instead, as
quinoa can be expensive. Always remember to wash all
grains thoroughly before use to get rid of any dirt. High in
lycopene, vitamin C, dietary fibre, essential fats and protein.
Low GL.

Preheat the oven to 170°C/gas mark 3/325°F.

Cut the tomatoes in half and deseed them with a small
knife, then toss them in a colander with 1 teaspoon of salt
and some black pepper, and set in the sink to drain for
15 minutes (the salt will draw moisture from the tomatoes).

Arrange the tomatoes in a single layer in a lipped baking
tray with the garlic cloves scattered around. Drizzle with the
rapeseed oil and roast for about 1 hour, until the tomatoes
are shrivelled and sweet and the garlic is squishy.

Meanwhile, rinse the quinoa under cold running water
and drain. Bring the water to a boil in a small pot. Stir in
the quinoa and a pinch of salt. Reduce the heat, cover and
simmer for 15–20 minutes, until the quinoa is fluffy and
tender and all the water has been absorbed. Remove from
the heat, uncover and let it cool.

Place the garlic, tomatoes, spices and stock in a food
processor. Leave a little stock to swirl around the baking
tray to catch any leftovers and pour into the food processor.
Pulse on medium, stopping before the soup is completely
smooth – a little bite is good.

Transfer the soup to a saucepan with the quinoa. Simmer
for 10 minutes. Serve topped with feta, chives and some
cracked black pepper.

Roast Red
Pepper &
Tomato Soup
£4·50
Lentil
& Veg
Stew £5.

ROAST
RED PEPPER AND SWEET POTATO SOUP

SERVES: 6

SF GF DF NF V

Ingredients

600g sweet potatoes, peeled
 and cut into medium chunks
500g red peppers, cut in half
 and deseeded
5 large cloves of garlic,
 unpeeled
1 large sprig of fresh rosemary,
 leaves removed from the stem
5 tablespoons extra virgin olive
 oil
Himalayan fine rock salt and
 freshly ground black pepper
1 large onion, chopped
1.2 litres hot water
Freshly chopped coriander, to
 garnish (optional)

An immune-boosting soup for cold days and nights. High in vitamin C, plant protein, dietary fibre, essential fats, lycopene and allicin.

Preheat the oven to 220°C/gas mark 7/425°F.

In a large roasting tin, combine the sweet potatoes, peppers, garlic, rosemary and 3 tablespoons of olive oil. Sprinkle with some salt and pepper and mix well so that everything is coated with oil. Roast for 45 minutes to 1 hour, until the peppers are blistered, making sure to mix everything around every 15 minutes or so. It's okay for the skin of the peppers to turn black – this is actually what you want. You'll remove most of the skin later anyway.

About 15 minutes before your veggies are ready, heat the remaining 2 tablespoons of olive oil in a soup pot on a low heat. Add the chopped onion and cook slowly for 15 minutes so that it becomes sweet and golden. You don't want to brown the onion, you want to caramelise it. This will add even more beautiful flavour to this soup.

Remove your veggies from the oven and let them cool for approximately 10 minutes. At this point, bring the 1.2 litres of water to a boil in a pot or kettle to save time. When cool enough to touch, use your clean fingers or tongs to remove as much of the blistered pepper skin as you can. Don't worry if you don't get it all because the soup is going to be blended.

Squeeze the roasted garlic out of its skin and add it to the pot along with the rest of your veggies. Mix the veggies together with the onions, then add the boiled water to the pot and give it a stir. Add some more salt and pepper.

Blend until smooth with a hand-held blender in the pot or transfer to an upright blender.

Taste and add a little more salt and pepper if necessary. Serve immediately and garnish with freshly chopped coriander if you like.

SAUCES AND PURÉES

These sauces are a fantastic accompaniment to all kinds of vegetable, meat and fish dishes when using your favourite rice or noodles. They are pretty easy to put together and you can make them ahead of time and refrigerate them to save time during your busy week. These colourful purées will also really impress your friends and family when added to your Sunday roast and are lovely during the warm summer months as vegetarian pâtés with crackers.

TANGY,

TASTY ALMOND SAUCE

MAKES: 200ML

Ingredients

70g smooth almond butter

20g coriander leaves, finely chopped

2 cloves of garlic, peeled

Juice of 1 lime

2 tablespoons dark brown sugar

1 tablespoon finely chopped fresh root ginger

1 tablespoon sesame oil

1 teaspoon harissa paste

60ml tamari

2 tablespoons rice wine vinegar

Intense flavours in this dynamic sauce give new life to a simple bowl of cooked brown rice and vegetables. Toss with noodles and crisp vegetables and you have an instant lunch. High in plant protein, dietary fibre and essential fats.

Put all the ingredients from the almond butter through to the harissa paste into a blender. Blend until smooth. Add the tamari and rice wine vinegar, blend again and season to taste.

ITALIAN
TOMATO SAUCE

🍴 **MAKES: 400ML**

Ingredients

1 x 400g can of whole plum
   tomatoes, chopped
60g fresh basil leaves
A few sprigs each of other
   fresh herbs (I love to use
   tarragon, coriander and
   chives plus a few leaves of
   parsley and thyme)
2 cloves of garlic, minced
Himalayan fine rock salt and
   freshly ground black pepper
3 tablespoons extra virgin
   olive oil
30g capers, preferably stored
   in salt
30g pitted black olives, sliced
1 fresh red chilli, deseeded
   and finely chopped (optional)

The fastest, easiest and most delicious pasta sauce is raw, takes 5 minutes to prepare and only calls for three main ingredients: ripe, juicy tomatoes, extra virgin olive oil and lots of fresh herbs. Oh, and your favourite pasta. High in lycopene, essential fats, dietary fibre, plant protein and allicin. Low GL.

Put the tomatoes into a large bowl with all of their juices – you need to use a large mixing or serving bowl so that you can add the hot pasta to the sauce and then serve it immediately.

Rinse all of your fresh ingredients well, especially if they've just been picked. Chop the herbs roughly and stir them into the tomatoes.

Add the minced garlic and season with salt and pepper, then stir in the olive oil, capers, olives and chilli. This sauce can be gently heated in a medium saucepan on a low to medium heat for 10 minutes or you can use it as is.

ALMOND
SATAY SAUCE

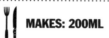 **MAKES: 200ML**

Ingredients
125g almond butter
125ml liquid aminos
60ml hot water
Juice of 1 orange
Juice of 1 lime
½ red chilli, deseeded and chopped
2 tablespoons finely chopped fresh
 coriander
1 tablespoon coconut oil
1 teaspoon grated fresh root ginger
½ teaspoon fish sauce

This is light and creamy, ideal for a salad dressing or for a chicken or monkfish rice dish. You'll love this one! High in plant protein, essential fats, dietary fibre and vitamin C. Low GL.

Put everything in a blender and blend for 15 seconds.

ULTIMATE
ASIAN SAUCE

 MAKES: 450ML

Ingredients
300ml water
60ml tamari
2 cloves of garlic, minced
2 tablespoons apple cider vinegar
2 tablespoons rice wine vinegar
1 tablespoon grated fresh root ginger
1 tablespoon honey
1 teaspoon toasted sesame oil
3 tablespoons fine maize meal

Great for a dipping sauce, stir-fry, salads and for marinating grilled meats and fish. High in allicin and dietary fibre.

Combine all the ingredients except the maize meal in a small bowl.

Place the fine maize meal in another small bowl and gradually whisk in the sauce until it's silky and smooth.

Transfer to a plastic airtight container and store in the fridge for up to three days to keep fresh. Heat gently in a small pot for a few minutes before using.

PUNCHY
PEANUT SAUCE

 MAKES: 200ML

Ingredients
125g smooth salt-free peanut
butter
120ml hot water
3 cloves of garlic, minced
2 tablespoons chopped fresh
coriander
2 tablespoons tamari
2 tablespoons honey
1 teaspoon apple cider vinegar
Pinch of ground turmeric
Pinch of Himalayan fine rock salt

This sauce is a fantastic dressing for Asian salads made with noodles or rice and vegetables, chicken, meat or seafood. High in plant protein, dietary fibre and essential fats.

Place the peanut butter in a bowl. Add the hot water and stir with a spoon until mixed.

Stir in the remaining ingredients and mix well. Use immediately, or it can be stored for up to a week in an airtight plastic container in the fridge.

PECAN
GINGER SAUCE

 MAKES: 300ML

Ingredients
400g pecans
250ml water
2 tablespoons grated fresh root
ginger
2 tablespoons honey
2 tablespoons apple cider vinegar
1 tablespoon tamari
½ teaspoon ground turmeric
½ teaspoon Himalayan fine rock salt

Ideal for rice or noodle stir-fries, or meat, fish or veggie dishes. High in magnesium, plant protein, essential fats and dietary fibre.

Preheat the oven to 150°C/gas mark 2/300°F.

Place the pecans on a baking tray and put in the oven for 15 minutes, then purée everything in a blender or food processor.

When the sauce is as smooth as you like it, use a spatula to remove from the blender and heat gently on a low heat before serving. It can be stored for up to a week in an airtight plastic container in the fridge.

ROASTED
RED PEPPER SAUCE

MAKES: 150ML

Ingredients
4 large red peppers
180ml extra virgin olive oil
1 clove of garlic, peeled
1 tablespoon finely chopped
  fresh thyme
1 tablespoon finely chopped
  fresh rosemary
1 tablespoon finely chopped
  fresh sage
1 teaspoon Himalayan fine rock
  salt
½ tablespoon freshly ground
  pepper

Red peppers contain lycopene and carotene, a phytochemical that offers protection against cancer and heart disease. It's the hit man of the vegetable world. High in dietary fibre, essential fats, lycopene and vitamin C. Low GL.

Preheat the oven to 200°C/gas mark 6/400°F.

Wash the peppers and pat them dry with a clean towel. Cut each pepper in half and remove the seeds. Brush both sides of each pepper with a little of the olive oil and lay them on a baking tray with the cut sides facing down. Grill the peppers in the oven for approximately 45 minutes, until the skins blister. Remove the peppers to a pot, cover the pot and refrigerate for 30 minutes.

In the meantime, heat 1 tablespoon of the olive oil in a large saucepan over a medium heat. Add the whole garlic clove and toast for 5 minutes, until golden. Remove from the heat and let it cool.

Peel the skin off the peppers and place them in a food processor. Add the garlic, herbs, salt and pepper. Turn on the food processor and slowly add the rest of the olive oil. Blend well for approximately 2 minutes, until smooth, and refrigerate for up to one week.

KALE
PURÉE

SF GF DF NF V

Ingredients

250g kale, stemmed, cleaned
and shredded
600ml water
1 clove of garlic, minced
1 teaspoon freshly squeezed
lemon juice
½ teaspoon Himalayan fine rock
salt
Pinch of freshly ground black
pepper

This is a delicious purée to use with grilled fish, homemade veggie burgers or bakes. You could even use it as a pasta sauce with pine nuts and feta cheese. Always wash your kale leaves thoroughly under cold running water to remove any dirt under the leaves. High in calcium, dietary fibre and plant protein. Low GL.

Remove the kale leaves from the tough stalk. Discard the stalk and cut the leaves into small pieces. Cook the kale with 300ml of boiling water in a covered wok or pot over a medium heat for 5 minutes, until tender and bright green.

Drain the kale and put it in a blender with the remaining 300ml of water, the garlic, lemon juice, salt and pepper. Purée until very smooth.

Scrape into a small bowl with a spatula and serve straight away, as this purée doesn't keep well overnight.

BEETROOT
PURÉE

 MAKES: 150ML

Ingredients
1 tablespoon rapeseed oil
2 fresh beetroots
120ml fresh apple juice
2 tablespoons freshly squeezed
  lemon juice
1 tablespoon apple cider vinegar
2 teaspoons honey
½ teaspoon Himalayan fine rock
  salt
Pinch of freshly ground black
  pepper
1 teaspoon fresh mint, chopped,
  to garnish

This purée works well as a garnish on soups and stews, and also on vegetarian burgers and bakes. The lemon in this recipe brightens the colour of the beetroot intensely, making it a real eye-catcher on the dinner table. High in folic acid, vitamin C, essential fats and dietary fibre.

Preheat the oven to 200°C/gas mark 6/400°F. Grease a baking tray with the rapeseed oil.

Scrub the beetroots in hot water and drain well. Place on the oiled baking tray and roast in the oven for 25 minutes, until tender. Cool to room temperature.

Rub the skins off the beetroots, then chop them into cubes and put them in a blender with the apple juice, lemon juice and vinegar. Purée until smooth.

Use a spatula to scrape the purée into a small bowl, then stir in the honey, salt and pepper.

Sprinkle the chopped mint on top to garnish.

SWEET POTATO
PURÉE

MAKES: 200ML

    SF GF DF NF V

Ingredients
1 tablespoon rapeseed oil
2 medium sweet potatoes,
  peeled and chopped into cubes
250ml water
3 tablespoons freshly squeezed
  orange juice
½ teaspoon freshly squeezed
  lemon juice
¼ teaspoon minced garlic
¼ teaspoon ground turmeric
¼ teaspoon grated fresh root
  ginger
Pinch of Himalayan fine rock salt
1 teaspoon fresh coriander,
  chopped, to garnish

This purée works well with any meat dishes, as it's hearty and warm. You could also use it on sandwiches, wraps and pittas as a dressing for lunchtime sambos. High in vitamin C, plant protein, dietary fibre and essential fats.

Preheat the oven to 200°C/gas mark 6/400°F.

Grease a baking tray with the rapeseed oil and spread out the sweet potatoes on it. Roast for 35 minutes, until tender. Remove from the oven and allow to cool for about 15 minutes.

Put the cooked sweet potatoes in a blender with all the other ingredients except the coriander and purée until very smooth. Use a spatula to scrape it into a small bowl. Garnish with the coriander.

HOMEMADE VEGGIE BURGERS

The best thing about making homemade veggie burgers is that you can use lots of yummy colourful vegetables, grains and pulses. Veggie burgers are an easy and effective way to get vital nutrients into fussy eaters and children. They also look and taste divine. You can refrigerate burgers for up to three days in an airtight container.

I've also included some ideas for sides and dips to serve with the burgers.

COURGETTE
AND BLUE CHEESE BURGERS

 MAKES: 8 LARGE BURGERS

Ingredients

700g floury potatoes,
unpeeled

Himalayan fine rock salt and
freshly ground black pepper

450g courgettes, grated and
drained

Rapeseed oil

200g blue cheese, crumbled

4 spring onions, finely
chopped

2 large eggs, beaten

4 tablespoons fresh mint,
chopped

2 tablespoons white spelt
flour

50g unsalted butter

Most of the nutrients, fibre and protein are found in the potato skin, so in this recipe I've left it in as it's so valuable to our health. High in dietary fibre, essential fats and protein. Low GL.

Preheat the oven to 170°C/gas mark 3/325°F.

Wash and scrub the potatoes, then boil them in a covered pot for 10 minutes on a medium to high heat until they are partially cooked. Drain and leave to cool.

Grate the potatoes using the large holes of a cheese grater into a large bowl and lightly season with some salt and pepper.

Toss the grated courgettes with a teaspoon of salt in a colander and spread the mixture evenly on a lightly oiled baking tray. Bake in the oven on the bottom shelf, stirring a few times, for 1 hour or until the courgettes reduce slightly in volume but are still moist. Remove from the oven and allow to cool completely.

Add the cooled courgettes to the grated potatoes along with the blue cheese, spring onions, beaten eggs and mint. Mix these all together with a wooden spoon.

With clean hands, divide the mixture into eight large patties. Lightly dust the burgers with the flour.

Heat a little butter in a large frying pan over a medium heat. Fry the burgers for about 5 minutes per side, until cooked through and golden on the outside. Repeat until all the burgers are ready to serve.

Serve in toasted floury baps with some pesto and green salad. Scrumptious stuff!

LENTIL
CASHEW BURGERS

🍴 **MAKES: 6**

Ingredients

145g red lentils, rinsed and
   drained

350ml water

2 tablespoons apple cider
   vinegar

1 tablespoon extra virgin olive oil

115g red onion, finely chopped

100g kale, washed and shredded

70g toasted cashew nuts, finely
   chopped

5 cloves of garlic, finely minced

1 teaspoon Dijon mustard

1 teaspoon Himalayan fine rock
   salt

30g oat bran

Rapeseed oil, for frying

I use locally grown kale in this recipe, which is full of calcium and magnesium. It also contains loads of chlorophyll, which is ideal for radiant, glowing skin. Once cooked, lentils can be stored in the refrigerator for up to three days in an airtight container. They are a good source of plant protein, folic acid, dietary fibre and vitamin C. Low GL.

Place the lentils and water in a small saucepan and bring to a boil. Lower the heat and simmer, partially covered, for about 25 minutes, until the lentils are soft and the liquid is absorbed.

Use a spatula to scrape the lentils into a medium-sized bowl. Add the apple cider vinegar and mash well.

Heat the olive oil in a wok over a low heat. Add the onion and sauté for 7 minutes, until softened. Add all remaining ingredients except the oat bran and sauté for 7 minutes more, until all the vegetables are tender. Add to the lentils with the oat bran and mix well. Leave to stand for 1 hour, until cool.

Form six medium-sized burgers with clean hands. Heat a little rapeseed oil in a large frying pan over a medium heat. Fry the burgers for about 5 minutes per side, until cooked through and golden on the outside.

SPICY

BEAN BURGERS

🍴 **MAKES: 5**

Ingredients

450g dried butter beans

2 tablespoons bicarbonate of soda

Extra virgin olive oil

8 spring onions, sliced lengthways into long strips

2 fresh red chillies, deseeded and thinly sliced

1 clove of garlic, crushed

20g fresh tarragon, finely chopped

½ teaspoon Himalayan fine rock salt

1½ tablespoons freshly squeezed lemon juice

150g feta cheese, crumbled

2 teaspoons sumac

Sumac is a tangy spice made from dried fruits, which tastes of lemon. You can buy it in your local health-food shop or gourmet store. High in protein, essential fats and dietary fibre. Low GL.

Place the butter beans in a large bowl and add twice their volume of cold water and the bicarbonate of soda. Leave to soak overnight.

The following day, drain the beans, place them in a large pan and cover with plenty of fresh water. Bring to a boil, then reduce the heat and simmer, covered, for at least 30 minutes, until soft to bite. This could take up to 1 hour, depending on the size of the beans. Add more water during cooking if necessary. When they're done, drain the beans.

Heat a little olive oil in a large frying pan over a medium heat. Add enough beans to cover the bottom of the pan and lightly fry them for 1–2 minutes on each side, until brown and blistered. Remove to a large bowl and continue with another batch of oil and beans.

When cooking the last batch, as soon as the beans are almost done, add the spring onions, chillies, garlic and tarragon. Sauté for about 1 minute. Add the rest of the beans to the pan, remove from the heat and season with the salt. Allow the beans to cool down. Taste for seasoning, then drizzle the lemon juice on top. Scatter the crumbled feta and the sumac over the top. Finish with a drizzle of olive oil and mix everything together well.

Heat a little olive oil in a large frying pan over a low to medium heat. Use a tablespoon to lift the burger mix into the pan and flatten it with the back of the spoon to create a not-too-perfect disc roughly 5cm x 1cm. Fry the burgers in batches for about 6 minutes on each side, until they have a nice brown crust. Place between two sheets of kitchen paper to soak up any excess oil. Serve hot or warm with salad or one of the homemade dips.

SWEET POTATO
CHICKPEA BURGERS

 MAKES: 6

Ingredients

1kg sweet potatoes, peeled and
 cut into large chunks
1 x 400g can of chickpeas,
 drained and rinsed
150g brown rice syrup
100g spelt flour
2 fresh red chillies, deseeded
 and finely chopped
3 tablespoons spring onions,
 chopped
2 teaspoons tamari
1 teaspoon Himalayan fine rock
 salt
Rapeseed oil, for frying

For the sauce

2 tablespoons extra virgin olive
 oil
1 tablespoon freshly squeezed
 lemon juice
1 tablespoon fresh coriander,
 chopped
Himalayan fine rock salt and
 freshly ground black pepper to
 taste

The darker the sweet potato, the greater the nutrients such as vitamin C, B vitamins, essential fats and dietary fibre in this action-packed vegetable.

Boil the sweet potatoes for 20 minutes, until soft, then leave in a colander to drain for 1 hour.

Meanwhile, whisk together all the sauce ingredients until smooth. Set aside.

Once the sweet potatoes have lost most of their liquid, place them in a mixing bowl and add the rest of the burger ingredients except the oil. Mix together by hand until it's smooth and even. Do not over-mix – it should be sticky. If it's too runny, add a little more flour.

Heat a little oil in a large frying pan over a medium heat. Use a tablespoon to lift the burger mix into the pan and flatten it with the back of the spoon to create a not-too-perfect disc roughly 5cm x 1cm. Fry the burgers in batches for about 6 minutes on each side, until they have a nice brown crust. Place between two sheets of kitchen paper to soak up any excess oil. Serve hot or warm with the sauce on the side.

SELECT STORES

QUINOA BURGERS

 MAKES: 4

Ingredients

250g quinoa

500ml water

Pinch of Himalayan fine rock salt

1 teaspoon gluten-free vegetable
 bouillon powder

70g amaranth grain

70g sesame seeds

1 small carrot, grated

1 red pepper, chopped

20g fresh flat-leaf parsley,
 chopped

Dash of tamari

Pinch of chilli powder

1 egg, beaten

Rapeseed oil, for frying

Sweet potato fries, to serve

Pesto, to serve

Quinoa is a gluten-free grain that contains an abundant amount of calcium and magnesium, which are beneficial for bone and brain health, making us all even more clever and fit! The fibre and nutrients in amaranth may reduce cholesterol, inflammation and high blood pressure, making it an all-around good food for heart health. High in protein, dietary fibre and essential fats. Low GL.

Rinse the quinoa under cold running water and drain. Bring the water to a boil in a small pot. Stir in the quinoa and a pinch of salt with the vegetable bouillon powder, adding the amaranth after 3–5 minutes. Reduce the heat, cover and simmer for 15–20 minutes, until the quinoa is fluffy and tender and all the water has been absorbed. Remove from the heat, uncover and let it cool a little.

Add the sesame seeds, carrot, red pepper, parsley, tamari and chilli powder. Mix in the beaten egg so the mixture lightly binds together, then form into four large burgers.

Heat a little rapeseed oil in a large frying pan over a low to medium heat. Fry the burgers for 5 minutes on each side, until golden and cooked through.

Serve with sweet potato fries and pesto (see pages 169–70 for recipes). These burgers keep well in the fridge and are a great snack or light lunch the next day.

SIDES AND DIPS FOR BURGERS

SWEETCORN
FRITTERS

Ingredients

125g white spelt flour

2 tablespoons polenta or
  medium maize/cornmeal

1 teaspoon baking powder

1 teaspoon date syrup or honey

2 eggs

1 egg yolk

125ml milk or milk alternative,
  such as oat milk

2 tablespoons crème fraîche

30g unsalted butter or butter
  alternative, such as soya spread

1 x 400g can of sweetcorn, rinsed
  and drained well

1 red chilli, deseeded and finely
  chopped

½ red onion, finely chopped

1 tablespoon coriander and/or
  chives, chopped

Himalayan fine rock salt and
  freshly ground black pepper

2 teaspoons rapeseed oil

Sweetcorn is popular with children, which is good as it's full of essential fatty acids, B vitamins and fibre – proper brain fuel. High in essential fats, protein, B vitamins and dietary fibre.

Put the flour, polenta, baking powder and syrup or honey in a bowl. Add the whole eggs and the egg yolk and beat together. Gradually beat in the milk and crème fraîche until you get a thick, smooth batter.

Heat half of the butter in a large frying pan until it turns brown and add it to the batter along with the sweetcorn, chilli, red onion and herbs, and season well.

Heat the oil and the remaining butter in a frying pan until quite hot. Drop tablespoonfuls of the fritter mixture into the pan and fry over a medium heat for about 2 minutes on each side, until golden brown. Serve immediately.

BROWN RICE
AND LEEK FRITTERS

SERVES: 4

Ingredients
350ml water

220g brown rice

3 leeks, trimmed

150ml extra virgin olive oil

5 shallots, finely chopped

1 fresh red chilli, deseeded and
 sliced

25g fresh flat-leaf parsley, finely
 chopped

1 teaspoon ground cumin

¾ teaspoon ground coriander

¼ teaspoon ground cinnamon

Pinch of Himalayan fine rock salt

1 egg white

1 egg

120g gluten-free self-raising flour

For the sauce
30g fresh coriander leaves, finely
 chopped

20g fresh flat-leaf parsley leaves,
 finely chopped

2 cloves of garlic, crushed

3 tablespoons olive oil

2 tablespoons freshly squeezed
 lime juice

½ teaspoon Himalayan fine rock
 salt

Leeks have similar health benefits to onions and garlic. They improve the immune system and are full of minerals that apparently work wonders for throat health. They are recommended by the greatest tenors and sopranos around. High in protein, dietary fibre and essential fats. Low GL.

Bring the water to a boil in a medium-sized saucepan and add the brown rice. Reduce to a simmer and cook, covered, for 30–40 minutes, until the rice is fluffy. Add more water if necessary.

Cut the leeks into 2cm-thick slices, rinse well and pat dry. Heat 75ml of the oil in a large frying pan on a low heat. Sauté the leeks and shallots for about 15 minutes, until completely softened. Transfer to a large bowl and add the cooked brown rice, chilli, parsley, spices and pinch of salt. Allow to cool.

In a spotlessly clean, dry bowl, whisk the egg white to soft peaks, then fold it into the vegetables. In another bowl, mix together the whole egg and the flour to form a batter. Gently mix it into the egg white and vegetable mixture.

Put 2 tablespoons of the remaining oil in a large frying pan and place over a medium heat. Spoon about half of the vegetable mixture into the pan to make four large fritters. Fry them for 3 minutes on each side, until golden and crisp. Transfer to a plate lined with kitchen paper and keep warm. Continue making more fritters, adding more oil as needed.

To make the sauce, put all the ingredients in a small bowl and stir with a tablespoon until mixed thoroughly.

Serve the fritters warm with the sauce on the side or drizzled over.

SWEET POTATO
FRIES

 SERVES: 4

Ingredients

4 medium sweet potatoes

4 teaspoons rapeseed or melted
 coconut oil

½ teaspoon Himalayan fine rock
 salt

¼ teaspoon freshly ground black
 pepper

You can enjoy this treat guilt free since the fries are baked, not deep-fried. Baking at this high temperature requires a little extra attention, but it will be worth it. Serve simply with just sea salt and pepper, or season using a blend of 1–2 teaspoons of ground spices, such as ginger, paprika or cinnamon. High in vitamin C, essential fats, dietary fibre and plant protein.

Preheat the oven to 230°C/gas mark 8/450°F.

Peel the potatoes and cut into fingers about ½cm wide. Place in a large bowl and add the oil, salt and pepper, tossing until coated. Spread the potatoes on two large baking sheets in a single layer.

Bake for 15 minutes, then rotate the baking sheets and gently turn over the potatoes. Continue baking for about 20 minutes, until the fries are crisp. Watch the potatoes closely and turn them frequently so they don't burn or stick to the pan. Serve immediately.

These are gorgeous with any of the dips from the next few pages.

TRADITIONAL

PESTO

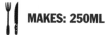 **MAKES: 250ML**

Ingredients

120g fresh basil leaves

40g raw cashews

2 cloves of garlic, peeled

120ml extra virgin olive oil, or as
needed

50g Parmesan, finely grated

A big bunch of beautiful basil is simply impossible to resist, and pesto is a delicious way to use it if you have large amounts. If you store it carefully (the layer of oil is all-important to prevent oxidisation), pesto will keep in the fridge for up to a month. You can even freeze it, but if you do, leave out the Parmesan and stir it through after it has defrosted. This version uses cashews because they are more economical than traditional pine nuts, but feel free to splurge if you want to. Almonds or pistachios also work a treat.

Use pesto on sandwiches or burgers, drizzle it over minestrone or your favourite salad, or serve it with grilled or roasted veggies. Or, if it's super fresh, simply toss it with hot pasta and enjoy! High in protein, essential fats and dietary fibre. Low GL.

Pulse the basil leaves, cashews and garlic in a food processor until they are finely chopped but not overworked. You'll need to scrape down the sides once or twice.

With the motor running, add the olive oil in a thin stream and stop when the consistency is correct: it should be like a thin spread. Stir in the Parmesan.

Decant the pesto into a clean jar and store in the fridge with a thin layer of oil poured on top to protect the surface.

SELECT STORES
VEGAN PESTO

 **MAKES: 200ML**

Ingredients

70g pine nuts

70g walnuts

3 cloves of garlic, peeled

80g fresh basil leaves

120ml extra virgin olive oil

2 tablespoons nutritional yeast

½ teaspoon Himalayan fine rock salt

½ teaspoon freshly ground black pepper

The nutritional yeast in this rich, vibrant green pesto lends a flavour similar to that of Parmesan cheese in traditional pesto. Serve over pasta, whole grains, or steamed or grilled veggies. High in vitamin E, plant protein, dietary fibre and essential fats. Low GL.

Pulse the pine nuts and walnuts in a food processor until finely chopped.

Add the garlic and pulse a few more times to blend.

Add the basil in batches, pulsing after each addition.

Add the olive oil, nutritional yeast, salt and pepper and pulse again until the pesto is creamy and well combined.

Keep in the fridge in an airtight container or glass jar, topped with a thin film of extra virgin olive oil, for up to ten days.

BEETROOT

HUMMUS

 MAKES: 450G

Ingredients

1 x 400g can of chickpeas,
 drained and rinsed

250g vacuum-packed beetroot

1 clove of garlic, crushed

100ml extra virgin olive oil

Juice of ½ lemon

2 tablespoons light tahini

2 teaspoons ground cumin

½ teaspoon Himalayan fine rock
 salt

Finely chopped fresh flat-leaf
 parsley, to garnish (optional)

Beetroot has always been used for medicinal purposes, especially for stimulating the liver with the detoxification process. High in folic acid, calcium, essential fats, dietary fibre and plant protein. Low GL.

Pop everything except the parsley into a blender or food processor and blend for 30 seconds, until the hummus has a chunky consistency. Transfer to a serving bowl and garnish with the chopped parsley.

Hummus will keep for up to five days stored in an airtight container or glass jar in the fridge.

HOW TO PREPARE
DRIED BEANS AND PEAS

Soaking whole dry pulses is essential for culinary and nutritional reasons. Soaking encourages even, complete cooking, helps break down hard-to-digest sugars (meaning less gas!), preserves nutrients and neutralises so-called anti-nutrients like phytic acid, which hinder the body's absorption of vital minerals.

1   Cover the pulses with plenty of cool water.

2   Leave in a moderately temperate place for about 8 hours or overnight, depending on size.

3   Drain the pulses and rinse thoroughly.

4   To cook, place the pulses in a pot and cover with three times the volume of cold water. Bring to a boil and simmer until tender, skimming off any froth that comes to the surface. This could take anywhere from 10 minutes to 1 hour, depending on what you're cooking. Small lentils cook very quickly, while beans and chickpeas take much longer.

CLASSIC
HUMMUS

🍴 **MAKES: 250G**

Ingredients

400g dried chickpeas

5 tablespoons dark tahini paste

3 tablespoons freshly squeezed
 lemon juice

2 tablespoons extra virgin olive
 oil

1 teaspoon smoked paprika

1 teaspoon tamari

Pinch of Himalayan fine rock salt

When making your own hummus from scratch, it's always best to use dried beans that you soak overnight. This leads to a creamier, more wholesome hummus that you'll love making again and again. High in calcium, plant protein, essential fats, dietary fibre and vitamin C. Low GL.

Soak the dried chickpeas overnight in plenty of water in an airtight container in a moderately temperate place.

The following day, drain the chickpeas and rinse thoroughly. Place in a large saucepan, cover with three times their volume of cold water and bring to a boil, then reduce to a simmer and cook for 1 hour, until tender.

Drain and add to a blender with all the remaining ingredients. Blend together, adding water as needed to reach your desired consistency. You will probably need to stop the blender several times to scrape down the sides. Add more smoked paprika, salt, lemon juice or tahini to taste.

Transfer to an airtight container or a glass jar, cover and refrigerate for several hours before serving. This hummus will last for up to five days in the fridge.

DINNERS

Try to have your dinner earlier in the evening if you can, as it aids digestion. The later you have dinner, the less nutrients will be absorbed as your digestive system is slowly shutting down to rest. If you eat late at night it can also lead to uncomfortable sleep, indigestion or gas.

I like to keep dinnertime preparation to a minimum, as sitting down and enjoying the meal is much more satisfying. It's the time of the day to chat about what went on or where things are going, and a good home-cooked meal is always the best foundation for the best conversations around the table. *Bon appétit*!

LENTIL

CHILLI

Ingredients

2 unsalted, gluten-free vegetable
 bouillon stock cubes

2 litres water

1 medium yellow onion, chopped

1 large red pepper, chopped

5 cloves of garlic, finely chopped

4 teaspoons salt-free chilli powder

500g brown lentils

2 x 400g cans of chopped tomatoes

20g fresh coriander, chopped

This simple vegetarian chilli recipe uses lentils instead of beans. Brown lentils work best, as they will hold their shape even when tender after cooking. High in dietary fibre, B vitamins, lycopene, allicin and plant protein. Low GL.

Add the vegetable bouillon stock cubes to 2 litres of boiling water and stir.

Bring 150ml of this broth to a simmer in a large pot over a medium to high heat. Add the onion, pepper and garlic and cook for about 8 minutes, until the onion is translucent and the pepper is tender.

Stir in the chilli powder and cook for 1 minute, stirring constantly. Add the lentils, tomatoes and remaining vegetable broth. Bring to a boil, then reduce the heat to medium to low and simmer, partially covered, for 30 minutes, until the lentils are almost tender. Uncover and cook for 10 minutes longer.

Stir in the coriander and serve.

LIVING

DAHL

🍴 **SERVES: 4**

Ingredients

1 tablespoon coconut oil

1 large onion, diced

4 cloves of garlic, finely chopped

1 tablespoon grated fresh root
ginger

½ bunch of fresh coriander, leaves
reserved, roots and stems finely
chopped

1 cinnamon stick

8 cardamom pods, crushed

1 teaspoon yellow mustard seeds

2 teaspoons ground coriander

2 teaspoons paprika

1 teaspoon ground cumin

½ teaspoon ground turmeric

½ teaspoon ground ginger

½ teaspoon chilli powder

½ teaspoon Himalayan fine rock salt

400g split red lentils, soaked (see
page 174)

400g sweet potatoes, peeled and
chopped into large medallions

1½ litres water

150g baby spinach

Natural yoghurt, to serve (optional)

Pitta bread or short-grain brown
rice, to serve

**Get your spice rack ready! This dahl takes about 40
minutes to make and you can refrigerate, once cooled, for
up to three days to eat on weeknights if you're too tired to
cook. Ah bliss!**

**Always remember spices and herbs can have an
alkalising effect on the body. So they are terrific for
glowing skin, nails and hair, plus good digestion. High in
magnesium, iron, B vitamins, plant protein, essential fats
and dietary fibre.**

Warm the coconut oil in a large saucepan over a low to
medium heat. Add the onion and cook, stirring, for 5–8
minutes, until softened.

Add the garlic, ginger, coriander roots and stems,
cinnamon stick, crushed cardamom and mustard seeds,
and cook for 2 minutes, stirring. Add the remaining spices
and the salt and cook for 1 minute more, stirring.

Add the lentils, sweet potatoes and water to the saucepan
and bring to a boil over a high heat. Reduce the heat to
low and allow the dahl to simmer for 15–20 minutes, until
the lentils have collapsed and the sweet potatoes are
tender. Take off the heat and stir through the spinach and
most of the coriander leaves.

Serve with a spoon of natural yoghurt on top, steamed
brown rice and garnish with the remaining coriander
leaves, chopped.

CHILLI
NON CARNE

🍴 **SERVES: 2**

SOY SF GF DF NF V

Ingredients

1 tablespoon extra virgin olive oil

1 large onion, chopped

2 cloves of garlic, crushed

2 x 400g cans of chopped
 tomatoes

1 x 400g can of pinto beans,
 drained, rinsed and mashed

200g Quorn mince (for a non-
 veggie option, use beef or lamb
 mince)

1 red pepper, chopped

1 teaspoon chilli powder

½ teaspoon Himalayan fine rock
 salt

½ teaspoon freshly ground black
 pepper

Sprinkle of nutritional yeast

I use pinto beans to give this chilli a delightfully creamy texture. High in plant protein, dietary fibre, essential fats, lycopene and allicin. Low GL.

Heat the olive oil in a large wok over a low to medium heat. Sauté the onion and garlic for 5–8 minutes, until softened.

Add the chopped tomatoes, mashed pinto beans, Quorn mince, red pepper, chilli powder, salt and pepper. Simmer, covered, for 30 minutes on a low heat.

Eat straight out of a bowl or with tortilla chips. Top with a sprinkle of nutritional yeast or make tacos with chopped onions, shredded lettuce and grated vegan cheese. This is also gorgeous with brown or white basmati rice.

MEDITERRANEAN
CHICKPEA STEW

SERVES: 4

SF · GF · DF · NF · VG

Ingredients

2 medium leeks

2 tablespoons extra virgin olive
 oil

1½ teaspoons ground coriander

1 teaspoon ground cumin

1 teaspoon ground fennel seed

½ teaspoon Himalayan fine rock
 salt

⅛ teaspoon cayenne pepper

1 x 400g can of chopped
 tomatoes with their juices

1 x 400g can of chickpeas, rinsed
 and drained

12 Kalamata or green olives,
 pitted and chopped

Zest of 1 lemon

1 tablespoon freshly squeezed
 lemon juice

Cooked millet or basmati rice, or
 wholewheat bread, to serve

80g feta cheese, broken into
 small pieces, to garnish
 (optional)

Vitamin C is a huge help when it comes to absorbing iron from plant sources. When beans (a good source of iron) are cooked with tomatoes (a good source of vitamin C), the combination can double the absorption of iron. This is easy to prepare and a delight to devour! We've made this several times to rave reviews at Select Stores. High in protein, vitamin C, dietary fibre, essential fats and protein. Low GL.

Trim the leeks, slit them in half lengthwise and rinse well under running water to remove any sand or grit. Coarsely chop the leeks.

Heat the oil in a large saucepan over a medium heat. Add the leeks, coriander, cumin, fennel seed, salt and cayenne pepper. Cook, stirring often, for about 5 minutes, until the leeks are soft.

Add the tomatoes with their liquid, the chickpeas, olives and lemon zest and bring to a boil. Reduce the heat to medium to low and cook, stirring occasionally, for about 15 minutes, until the tomato sauce is very thick. Remove from the heat and stir in the lemon juice.

Serve immediately over cooked millet or rice, or with wholewheat bread, and garnish with the feta cheese if you wish.

HEARTY WINTER
RED LENTIL CURRY

SERVES: 5

Ingredients

1 cauliflower, cut into florets
3 tablespoons coconut oil, melted
½ teaspoon fenugreek seeds
½ teaspoon black mustard seeds
1 medium onion, chopped
1½ teaspoons ground cumin
1 teaspoon ground coriander
1 teaspoon ground turmeric
1 teaspoon chilli powder
2 cloves of garlic, minced
1 teaspoon grated fresh root ginger
Himalayan fine rock salt
400g dried red lentils, rinsed and drained
1 x 400g can of chopped tomatoes
1.2 litres water
Freshly ground black pepper
Cooked brown rice, to serve
Chopped fresh coriander, to garnish

This is an exceptional vegan dinner – even the meat eaters out there will fall in love with this dish. High in dietary fibre, essential fats, plant protein and B vitamins. Low GL.

Preheat the oven to 200°C/gas mark 6/400°F.

Lay the cauliflower florets on a baking sheet and toss with 2 tablespoons of the coconut oil. Roast for approximately 30 minutes, turning them a few times throughout the cooking time until golden.

Heat the remaining tablespoon of coconut oil in a large pot on a low to medium heat. Add the fenugreek and mustard seeds. Fry for 5 minutes, until they start to pop.

Add the chopped onion and stir. Simmer gently for 5 minutes, until translucent.

Add the ground cumin, coriander, turmeric, chilli powder, garlic, ginger and a few pinches of salt to the pot. Mix well and simmer gently for 5 minutes. If the base of the pot is a little dry, just add a little water.

Stir in the lentils. Mix and spice it up for 3 minutes.

Add your chopped tomatoes and the water. Cover and bring to a boil.

Once it comes to a boil, reduce the heat to medium to low and simmer for 30 minutes, adding more water if necessary near the end.

Once the lentils have collapsed they are cooked. Remove the pot from the heat and add the roasted cauliflower. Season with salt and pepper.

Serve with brown rice and garnish with chopped coriander. Namaste!

PUMPKIN

AND FETA PEARL BARLEY RISOTTO

 SERVES: 4

Ingredients

1 tablespoon unsalted butter

1 medium courgette, quartered lengthways and chopped into thick pieces

600g pumpkin or butternut squash, peeled and chopped into cubes

2 cloves of garlic, crushed

Zest of 1 lemon

1 tablespoon chopped fresh thyme leaves

5 tablespoons dry white wine

1 unsalted, gluten-free vegetable bouillon stock cube

1 litre hot water

300g pearl barley, rinsed and drained

Himalayan fine rock salt and freshly ground black pepper

80g frozen peas

100g feta cheese, crumbled

Rocket leaves, to serve

I've been using pearl barley in risotto ever since I made a green vegetable risotto last year. I love the hearty, wholesome texture and flavour that the barley lends to the dish. Note that the pearl barley takes a little longer to cook than Arborio rice – about 30 minutes instead of 15 minutes. High in selenium, dietary fibre and protein. Low GL.

Melt the butter in a deep frying pan over a medium to low heat. Add the courgette and cook for 2–3 minutes, until softened. Add the pumpkin or squash, garlic, half of the lemon zest and half of the thyme, stirring to coat. Add the wine, cover, and cook for 10 minutes, until the pumpkin is almost cooked.

Meanwhile, add the bouillon stock cube to 1 litre of hot water and stir. Bring this vegetable broth to a boil in a saucepan and keep it simmering over a low heat.

Add the pearl barley to the pumpkin mixture and stir for 1–2 minutes to coat the grains. Add the hot broth one ladleful at a time. Wait for the broth to be fully absorbed before adding more. Continue for 20–30 minutes, stirring constantly, until all the broth has been absorbed and the barley is cooked through and slightly firm to the bite.

Season to taste, then stir in the peas and half of the feta. Serve topped with the remaining lemon zest, thyme, feta and rocket.

SWEET POTATO
AND QUINOA CURRY

🍴 **SERVES: 4**

Ingredients

2 tablespoons extra virgin olive
 oil

1 large red onion, finely chopped

1 clove of garlic, minced

1 teaspoon grated fresh root
 ginger

1 unsalted, gluten-free vegetable
 or chicken stock cube (optional)

400ml hot water

2 medium sweet potatoes,
 peeled and diced

1 x 400g can of chickpeas,
 drained and rinsed

200g quinoa

1 tablespoon mild curry powder

1 tablespoon ground cumin

80g baby spinach

Himalayan fine rock salt and
 freshly ground black pepper

When making broth, I usually use organic, low-salt, no-yeast, gluten-free brands like Kallo or Marigold, which you can find in your local health-food shop or supermarket. High in plant protein, dietary fibre, essential fats and B vitamins.

Heat the olive oil in a large pan over a low to medium heat. Add the onion, garlic and ginger and cook for 5–8 minutes, until softened.

Dissolve the stock cube (if using) in 400ml of hot water in a Pyrex jug. Add the broth or water, sweet potatoes, chickpeas, quinoa, curry powder and cumin to the pan. Bring to a boil, then reduce the heat and cover.

Simmer for 20 minutes, until the quinoa and sweet potatoes are cooked through. Add a little water if the liquid evaporates before the quinoa is fully cooked.

Add the spinach and stir well. Cover again and cook just until the spinach has wilted. Add salt and pepper if desired.

CITRUS CASHEW
NUT MILLET WITH BROCCOLI

 🍴 **SERVES: 4**

Ingredients

1 tablespoon extra virgin olive oil

2 shallots, peeled and finely
 diced

½ red onion, peeled and finely
 chopped

2 cloves of garlic, minced

1 unsalted, gluten-free vegetable
 bouillon stock cube

240ml hot water

60g sun-dried tomatoes,
 chopped

120ml white wine

2 tablespoons freshly squeezed
 lemon juice

200g millet

½ teaspoon Himalayan fine rock
 salt or to taste

200g broccoli florets, cut into
 bite-size pieces

Freshly ground black pepper

80g cashew nuts

A handful of minced fresh
 coriander

This one is for all the protein lovers out there. There is 23g of plant protein in 200g of millet. So this dish is perfect after you return home from the gym looking for sustenance. Plus, you'll enjoy a burst of flavours and textures. High in plant protein, dietary fibre, essential fats, calcium and magnesium.

Heat the olive oil in a saucepan over a medium heat. Sauté the shallots, onion and garlic for 3 minutes.

Dissolve the stock cube in the hot water in a Pyrex jug. Add this vegetable broth, the sun-dried tomatoes, wine and lemon juice to the saucepan and bring to a boil, then stir in the millet and salt. Reduce the heat and simmer, covered, for 15–20 minutes, until the millet is fluffy. Add more hot water if necessary.

Add the broccoli and simmer for 5–7 minutes longer, until the broccoli is tender. Remove from the heat, taste and adjust the seasoning with salt and pepper.

Toast the cashew nuts in a small frying pan for 3–5 minutes on a low to medium heat, until browned. Garnish the dish with the toasted cashews and coriander before serving.

SIMPLE VEGETABLE
AND QUINOA CASSEROLE WITH TOFU

SERVES: 4

Ingredients

185g quinoa

400ml water

350g plain tofu, cut into cubes

3 tablespoons tamari

4 tablespoons grapeseed oil

1 large onion, chopped

180g frozen peas

3 sticks of celery, chopped

2 carrots, cut into julienne strips

1 medium green pepper, cut into
 small pieces

2 large cloves of garlic

1 tablespoon chopped fresh flat-
 leaf parsley

1 teaspoon dried mixed herbs

1 tablespoon rice flour

1½ unsalted, gluten-free
 vegetable stock cubes

600ml hot water

2 tablespoons tomato purée

Steamed green beans and
 mangetout, to serve

There are many different varieties of quinoa. The most popular is the yellow kind, but orange, red and black are popular varieties too. Quinoa is rich in amino acids, so it's nutritious and tasty. High in plant protein, dietary fibre, essential fats, calcium and iron. Low GL.

Preheat the oven to 190°C/gas mark 5/375°F.

Wash the quinoa and drain it through a sieve, then place it in a saucepan with the water. Cover and bring to a boil, then reduce the heat and simmer for about 20 minutes, until the water has been absorbed.

Briefly marinate the tofu in 2 tablespoons of the tamari in a small mixing bowl. Heat 2 tablespoons of the grapeseed oil in a frying pan over a medium heat, then fry the tofu for 10 minutes, stirring occasionally, until lightly golden. Set aside to add to the casserole later.

Heat the remaining 2 tablespoons of grapeseed oil in a cast-iron casserole dish over a medium heat. Fry the onion for a few minutes, then add the frozen peas, celery, carrots, green pepper, garlic, parsley and mixed herbs and fry for a few minutes more.

Stir in the tablespoon of rice flour and cook for 1 minute, until all the vegetables are coated. Dissolve the stock cubes in 600ml of hot water in a Pyrex jug, then add to the casserole along with the tomato purée and the remaining tablespoon of tamari. Bring to a boil, then reduce the heat and simmer for 1 minute.

Transfer the casserole to the oven and bake for 30 minutes, until the vegetables are soft. Add the tofu and quinoa for a few minutes at the end. Serve with steamed green beans and mangetout.

SELECT STORES

IRISH LAMB STEW

SERVES: 4

Ingredients

4 tablespoons rapeseed oil

1kg lean Irish stewing lamb, cut into chunks (you can tenderise the meat by wrapping it in cling film and pounding it with a mallet)

2 large onions, sliced

1 red onion, sliced

1 clove of garlic, crushed

4 tablespoons white spelt flour

2 tablespoons cocoa powder

½ teaspoon Himalayan fine rock salt

½ teaspoon freshly ground black pepper

¼ teaspoon dried oregano

¼ teaspoon dried marjoram

850ml boiling water

150g carrots, diced

4 large floury potatoes, peeled and cut into chunks

1 teaspoon horseradish relish

This is my mammy's recipe, God rest her soul. She would always prepare this on very cold winter nights when your hands were cold, your nose was cold and your feet were cold. You would be warmed up in no time at all from the feet upwards. I know that using a little cocoa powder sounds weird, but it makes a really tasty stew with a lot of depth and character. You can buy horseradish relish in a gourmet or health-food shop in the chilled section. Lamb is an excellent source of protein, zinc, selenium and vitamin B12. High in protein, iron, B vitamins and dietary fibre. Low GL.

Heat the oil in a large frying pan over a medium heat, then add in the meat in batches and brown it on all sides. This should take about 10 minutes per batch. Remove the meat from the pan with a slotted spoon and set aside.

Add the onions and garlic to the frying pan and cook for 5–8 minutes, until soft. Remove from the pan with a slotted spoon and add the flour to the oil remaining in the pan. Add the cocoa, seasoning and herbs and stir until slightly thickened.

Return the meat, onions and garlic to the pan along with the boiling water. Cover and bring to a boil, then reduce the heat and simmer for about 45 minutes. Add the carrots, potatoes and horseradish relish and top up with additional water if necessary to cover the ingredients. Simmer for another 30 minutes, until the carrots and potatoes are tender. Serve hot.

VEGAN

VEGETABLE KORMA

SERVES: 4

Ingredients

1 tablespoon coconut oil

1 tablespoon sliced almonds

1 tablespoon garlic, chopped

1 tablespoon roughly chopped fresh root
 ginger

1 tablespoon ground cumin

2 teaspoons ground turmeric

2 teaspoons ground coriander

1 teaspoon ground cinnamon

1 teaspoon freshly ground cardamom
 seeds

3 whole star anise

300g coconut cream or natural coconut
 yoghurt

225g fresh pineapple (optional)

1 tablespoon dark brown sugar

1 tablespoon freshly squeezed lime juice

Himalayan fine rock salt

70g cauliflower, cut into small pieces

150g butternut squash, peeled and cut
 into small pieces

70g courgette, cut into small pieces

70g aubergine, cut into small pieces

70g broccoli, cut into small florets

250ml water

Cooked brown or white rice, roasted
 papadums and mango chutney, to serve

This is a recipe that I love to make when I'm stuck for time. I make it in bulk as it will keep refrigerated in a sealed plastic container for up to three days once cooled, so it's ideal for families, students or singles on the go. Star anise is very medicinal, with powerful antibacterial qualities and high antioxidant levels. Rocket fuel! High in vitamin C, dietary fibre, essential fats and plant protein.

Place the coconut oil, almonds, garlic, ginger and spices in a small saucepan. Cook on a high heat, stirring regularly, for 3–5 minutes, until the almonds are golden. Add the coconut cream, pineapple (if using), sugar and lime juice. Bring to a boil, then reduce the heat and simmer for 15 minutes. Add salt to taste.

Put the vegetables and water in a large pan or wok and place over a medium heat. Add the spice and coconut mix and toss to combine. Cover and cook for about 30 minutes, until all the veggies are tender.

Remove the star anise before serving. Serve with steamed brown or white basmati rice with some roasted papadums and mango chutney.

CASHEW,
MANGO AND TOFU STIR-FRY

SERVES: 3

For the stir-fry
250g short-grain brown rice

400ml boiling water

1 tablespoon peanut oil

2 shallots, sliced

4 cloves of garlic, sliced

1 head of pak choi, sliced

1 spring onion, cut into julienne
strips

2 mangos, stoned and sliced

250g tofu, cut into cubes

60g toasted cashews

2 tablespoons chopped fresh
coriander

For the tamarind sauce
60ml shoyu sauce

60ml tamari

2 cloves of garlic, finely chopped

2 tablespoons tamarind paste

2 tablespoons honey

2 tablespoons grated fresh root
ginger

2 tablespoons freshly squeezed
lime juice

1 tablespoon sumac

Pinch of freshly ground black
pepper

120ml water

2 teaspoons fine maize meal

One of the most natural foods in South Asia, the tangy tamarind, which means 'date of India', is gaining recognition and appreciation throughout the world. High in vitamin C, essential fats, plant protein and dietary fibre.

Place the rice in a medium pot and cover with the boiling water. Simmer for 40 minutes, covered, adding a little more water if necessary, until the rice is cooked through and fluffy.

Meanwhile, to prepare the tamarind sauce, combine all the ingredients except the water and maize meal in a pot and bring to a boil. Simmer for 5 minutes. In a small bowl, mix the maize meal and water together, then add it to the sauce. Let it simmer for 10 minutes and set aside when it thickens.

Heat the peanut oil in a wok over a low to medium heat. Add the shallots and garlic and fry for 5–8 minutes, until golden. Add the pak choi and spring onion and fry for 4 more minutes. Add the mangos, tofu, cashews and half of the sauce. Simmer for 10 minutes, until all the ingredients are cooked through.

Add the rest of the sauce, then stir in the chopped coriander to finish. Serve immediately over the brown rice.

COCONUT GROVE
CHICKEN CURRY STIR-FRY

|| SERVES: 3

For the stir-fry

2 tablespoons coconut oil

500g chicken fillets, diced

400g broccoli florets

150g canned sliced water
  chestnuts, drained

Cooked brown basmati or short-
  grain brown rice, to serve

For the coconut curry sauce

2 tablespoons creamed coconut

2 tablespoons natural coconut
  yoghurt

20g toasted coconut flakes

2 large cloves of garlic

5 stalks of fresh coriander, finely
  chopped

1 small finger of fresh root
  ginger, grated

250ml water

2 tablespoons coconut oil

1½ tablespoons mild curry
  powder

1½ teaspoons Himalayan fine
  rock salt

Coconut oil has really taken off as the trendy new ingredient to use in the kitchen. It's great for stir-frying, as cooking it at high temperatures doesn't turn it into a nasty trans-fat. Other fabulous high-temperature cooking oils are sunflower, grapeseed and rapeseed. High in dietary fibre, protein, essential fats, selenium, vitamin C and B vitamins. Low GL.

To make the sauce, add all the ingredients to a blender or food processor and blend for 15 seconds.

Heat the coconut oil in a large pan over a medium heat. Add the chicken and brown it on all sides. Add the broccoli and water chestnuts along with the curry sauce and let it simmer for 20–25 minutes, stirring occasionally, until the chicken is cooked through.

Serve with brown basmati or short-grain brown rice and enjoy.

FULLY LOADED
PAELLA

🍴 **SERVES: 5**

C SOY SF GF DF NF V

Ingredients

3 tablespoons extra virgin olive oil

1 large onion, chopped finely

6 cloves of garlic, minced

½ teaspoon chilli flakes

Pinch of Himalayan fine rock salt

2 large yellow peppers, diced

1 x 400g can of whole plum tomatoes, roughly chopped

2 tablespoons chopped fresh thyme

1 teaspoon chilli powder

1 tablespoon paprika

250g Arborio rice

2 low-salt, gluten-free vegetable stock cubes

600ml hot water

225g edamame beans

15g fresh coriander, chopped

15g fresh flat-leaf parsley, chopped

Pinch of freshly ground black pepper

I use frozen edamame beans for this dish, which you can find in your local health-food shop or Asian market. They'll keep in your freezer for up to four months. They are very high in protein and lecithin, which may lower cholesterol. They're also lovely with seafood, chicken or beef. High in dietary fibre, essential fats, allicin, lycopene and plant protein. Low GL.

Heat the olive oil in a large wok over a low to medium heat. Sauté the onion, garlic, chilli flakes and a pinch of salt for 5–8 minutes, until the onions are soft. Add the yellow peppers, tomatoes, thyme, chilli powder and paprika and simmer, covered, for 10 minutes. Stir in the rice to coat it well.

Dissolve the stock cubes in the hot water in a Pyrex jug, then pour into the wok. Cover and reduce the heat to low. Cook until the rice is tender and most of the liquid has been absorbed. This should take about 25 minutes.

Add the edamame beans towards the end of the cooking time. Stir in the fresh herbs and season to taste with black pepper before dishing up.

SPAGHETTI

WITH COURGETTES, ANCHOVY, CHILLI AND LEMON

SERVES: 4

Ingredients

375g wholewheat spaghetti

2 tablespoons extra virgin olive oil

1 onion, chopped

2 cloves of garlic, finely sliced

250g canned anchovy fillets, drained

½ teaspoon chilli flakes

2 courgettes, grated

Zest and juice of 1 lemon

20g fresh flat-leaf parsley, chopped

Himalayan fine rock salt and freshly ground black pepper

70g baby rocket leaves

25g Parmesan, finely grated

For marathon runners and athletes who need a carb-heavy meal before race day, pasta is an excellent fuel. Ditto for those who do strenuous workouts where endurance is needed. The carbs serve as quick calories that the body can use for energy and burn off. This is why you want to avoid making pasta your daily dinner choice, because those carbs will be stored as fat if they aren't used, but once or twice a week is fine. Inspired by my visits to Monaco to see my friend Olivia Gaynor-Long and her sis Caitriona, this is light, low calorie, lightly spiced and really nice – yummy in the tummy. High in dietary fibre, essential fats and protein. Low GL.

Cook the pasta in boiling salted water according to the packet instructions. Drain well and place it back in the pan.

Meanwhile, heat the olive oil in a medium saucepan over a medium heat. Add the onion, garlic, anchovies and chilli flakes. Cook for 5 minutes, until the onion is soft. Add the grated courgettes, lemon zest and juice and parsley and cook for 2 minutes more. Season to taste.

Add the courgette mixture and the rocket to the drained pasta, tossing to combine. Serve the pasta topped with the grated Parmesan.

WHOLEGRAIN PENNE
WITH SALMON AND LEMON

 SERVES: 4

Ingredients

4 small salmon fillets

2 tablespoons rapeseed oil

½ teaspoon freshly grated lemon zest

¼ teaspoon freshly ground black pepper

225g 100% wholegrain penne pasta

200g fresh or frozen petit pois

300g baby spinach

30g fresh dill, chopped

2 tablespoons freshly squeezed lemon juice

¾ teaspoon crushed fennel seeds

Wholegrain pasta is healthier, heartier and tastier than white. This quick and easy pasta is a great weeknight recipe featuring the classic combination of salmon, peas and dill. High in essential fats, dietary fibre, calcium and protein. Low GL.

Preheat the oven to 180°C/gas mark 4/350°F. Bring a large pot of water to a boil for cooking the pasta.

Rub the salmon fillets with the oil. Place the salmon on a baking tray and sprinkle with the lemon zest and pepper. Cover the tray with aluminium foil and bake for 18–20 minutes, until the fish is cooked through.

Meanwhile, add the pasta to the boiling salted water and cook according to the packet instructions. Add the peas to the pasta 2 minutes before the pasta is done.

Drain the pasta and peas and return to the pot. Stir in the spinach, dill, lemon juice and fennel seeds and toss until well combined. Flake the salmon into bite-size pieces and scatter it over the pasta to serve.

WHOLEWHEAT PENNE
WITH KALE AND PRAWNS

🍴 SERVES: 6

Ingredients
500g frozen prawns
450g wholewheat penne
300g kale
30g sun-dried tomatoes, finely
 chopped
30g black olives, pitted and finely
 chopped
20g fresh basil, leaves chopped
10g fresh flat-leaf parsley,
 chopped
4 cloves of garlic, minced
3 tablespoons capers
2 tablespoons extra virgin olive
 oil
1 tablespoon balsamic vinegar
1 teaspoon chilli flakes
¼ teaspoon Himalayan fine rock
 salt
Pinch of freshly ground black
 pepper

Prawns are an excellent source of protein, the strong antioxidant selenium and vitamin B12. High in protein, dietary fibre, essential fats, calcium and vitamin C. Low GL.

Put the frozen prawns in a large pot set over a low heat. Cover the pot and cook for 8 minutes, stirring occasionally, until the prawns are cooked through, being careful not to overcook them. Drain the prawns and set aside.

Bring a large pot of salted water to a boil. Add the penne and cook for 10 minutes, until al dente, or according to the packet instructions.

Meanwhile, cut the kale leaves from the tough stalk. Discard the stalk and cut the leaves into small pieces. Add some of the starchy water from the pasta pot to a wok or large frying pan set over a medium heat. Add the kale and sun-dried tomatoes, cover and cook for 5 minutes, stirring occasionally.

In a medium bowl, combine the olives, herbs, garlic and capers, then stir in the olive oil, vinegar, chilli flakes, salt and pepper.

While the pasta continues to cook, add the olive oil mix and the prawns to the kale in the wok and stir for 1 minute. Add a little water if the sauce has all been absorbed. Cover the wok and keep warm.

When the pasta is cooked, drain and toss with the kale to mix well.

LOADED
STUFFED SWEET POTATOES

🍴 **SERVES: 2**

Ingredients

2 medium sweet potatoes,
scrubbed clean

130g canned black beans, rinsed
and drained well

80g canned sweetcorn

80g red pepper, diced

¼ teaspoon chilli powder

⅛ teaspoon ground cumin

Juice of 2 limes

2 tablespoons finely chopped
fresh coriander, plus extra to
garnish

1 tablespoon extra virgin olive oil

½ avocado, stoned, peeled and
diced

High in dietary fibre, essential fats and plant protein to help keep you full, this recipe also contains heaps of the antioxidants beta-carotene, lycopene, vitamin E and vitamin C.

Preheat the oven to 200°C/gas mark 6/400°F. Line a baking tray with foil.

Use a fork to prick holes in the sweet potatoes. Place on the foil-lined tray and bake in the oven for 45–50 minutes, until the flesh is soft.

Meanwhile, combine the black beans, sweetcorn and diced pepper in a bowl with the chilli powder, cumin and lime juice. In a separate small bowl, combine the chopped coriander with the olive oil. Set aside to let the flavours develop.

When the sweet potatoes are cooked, remove them from the oven and allow to cool slightly. Cut slits down each potato lengthwise and pull them apart so that you create a well for the fillings.

Into each potato, spoon 1½ tablespoons of the herby olive oil, followed by the corn and bean mixture. Top with diced avocado and extra chopped fresh coriander and serve immediately.

QUINOA

WITH CHILLI 'N' CHEESE

🍴 **SERVES: 7**

Ingredients

200g quinoa

400ml water

Himalayan fine rock salt

230ml cream

500g baby new potatoes

2 tablespoons extra virgin olive
  oil

1 medium onion, chopped

3 cloves of garlic, minced

225g canned chopped tomatoes

1–2 mild green chillies, deseeded
  and thinly sliced

2 tablespoons finely chopped
  fresh coriander

Freshly ground black pepper

180g mild Cheddar cheese,
  grated

This is a fun recipe to make whenever you are minding kids and it's raining outside. Just pop on a DVD of their favourite movie so you can 'let it go' in the kitchen and throw this together. Once they smell this dish, they'll appear. It's gorgeous with tacos and guacamole. High in protein, essential fats, dietary fibre, calcium and vitamin C. Low GL.

Rinse the quinoa under cold running water and drain. Bring the water to a boil in a small pot. Stir in the quinoa and a pinch of salt. Reduce the heat, cover and simmer for 15–20 minutes, until the quinoa is fluffy and tender and all the water has been absorbed. Remove from the heat, stir in the cream and set aside.

Meanwhile, in a separate saucepan, boil the potatoes in lightly salted water for 15–20 minutes, until just tender. Drain and cut into 2cm chunks when they are cool enough to handle.

Heat the olive oil in a deep frying pan over a medium heat. Add the onion and garlic and sauté for 5–8 minutes, until golden. Stir in the tomatoes, chillies and coriander. Add the quinoa and diced potatoes to the frying pan and gently fold together. Season to taste.

Fold in the cheese and serve directly from the frying pan.

OLLIE'S FUEL FOOD

VEGGIE BAKE

🍴 **SERVES: 2**

Ingredients

800ml water

2 low-salt, yeast-free, gluten-free vegetable stock cubes

200g brown lentils, washed and rinsed

200g millet, washed and rinsed

200g baby spinach

200g sweet potato, peeled and cubed

1 tablespoon harissa paste

1 teaspoon ground turmeric

2 tablespoons rapeseed oil

150g onions, diced

150g red peppers, diced

2 large cloves of garlic, minced

I love using layers of grains and vegetables when creating our popular vegetarian and vegan bakes for the deli. You could also add cooked marinated chicken, fish, lamb or beef as a layer to this dish if you like. High in plant protein, dietary fibre, essential fats and vitamin C.

Preheat the oven to 180°C/gas mark 4/350°F.

Boil the water and add the vegetable stock cubes. Stir to dissolve and leave to one side.

To begin with, you need three medium saucepans. In the first saucepan, cover the lentils with 400ml of the vegetable stock. Simmer for 25 minutes, until the stock has been soaked up and the lentils have collapsed. Add some more water and continue to cook for 10 minutes more, until the lentils are cooked through. Drain off any excess water in a colander or sieve and set aside.

Another saucepan is for the millet. Again, add 400ml of the vegetable stock and simmer for 15 minutes, until the stock has been soaked up by the millet. Add some water and continue to cook for 5 minutes more, until the millet is fluffy. Drain off any excess water in a colander or sieve and set aside.

While the millet is cooking, use a sieve to steam about 50g of the baby spinach over the saucepan. This will take 5 minutes. Set aside.

The last saucepan is for the sweet potatoes. Cover them with hot water and simmer for about 20 minutes, until soft. Drain and place the sweet potatoes back into the saucepan. Mash with the harissa paste and turmeric until you have a thick purée.

Now heat 1 tablespoon of the oil in a wok over a medium heat. Add the onions, peppers, the rest of the baby spinach and the garlic. Sauté for 5 minutes, until the vegetables are soft. Add a little water to the base of the wok if it looks too dry. Remove from the heat once the vegetables are soft.

This is the fun part: layering. Grab a medium-sized deep baking tray or dish and grease with the remaining tablespoon of oil. Add the millet as your base, using a spatula or wooden spoon to flatten it. Next add the vegetable mix on top of the millet, again flattening it. (This is where you could add some meat or fish if you wanted to as the next layer.) Add the lentils and flatten them, then top it off with the lightly spiced sweet potato mash. As you do so, mix the steamed baby spinach on top and create your own design.

Finally, pop the dish in the oven for 20 minutes, until the top is toasty. Cut servings with a large knife and serve with a spatula. It's beautiful with a salad of your choice.

FUEL FOOD
SHEPHERD'S PIE

Ingredients

675g lamb mince
Himalayan fine rock salt and
  freshly ground black pepper
Extra virgin olive oil
3 onions, chopped
3 bay leaves
1 tablespoon chopped fresh flat-
  leaf parsley
2 teaspoons fresh thyme leaves
1 tablespoon white spelt flour
2 tablespoons tomato purée
1 teaspoon harissa paste
2 tablespoons red wine
1 low-salt, gluten-free beef stock
  cube
225ml hot water
900g potatoes, peeled and
  quartered
1 carrot, finely chopped
50g unsalted butter
1 tablespoon milk

I love using harissa paste in my shepherd's pie to give it a little spicy edge and flavour. It also works very well with lamb. You can buy harissa paste in your local health-food shop, but if you can't find it, use chilli flakes instead. High in protein and dietary fibre.

Preheat the oven to 200°C/gas mark 6/400°F.

Season the mince with salt and pepper. Heat a little extra virgin olive oil in a large pan and cook the mince in small batches for a few minutes, until well coloured all over. Drain in a colander to remove the fat.

Heat a little more oil in the pan and gently fry the onions with the herbs for 5–8 minutes, until soft. Add the meat and dust with the flour, then add the tomato purée and harissa paste. Stir constantly and add the wine.

Dissolve the stock cube in the hot water in a Pyrex jug, then add it to the pan, mixing in well. Bring to a boil, then lower the heat and simmer for about 1 hour, until thickened. Adjust the seasoning, remove the bay leaves and set aside to cool. Skim off any oil that has risen to the surface.

Meanwhile, cook the potatoes and carrot in boiling salted water for 15 minutes, until tender, then drain and return to the pan briefly to dry. Mash the potatoes and carrot with the butter and milk and season well with salt and pepper.

Put the meat in one large baking dish or individual dishes and top with the mashed potatoes, roughing up the surface with a fork. Bake for 35–40 minutes, until the top is crusty and golden.

WILD SALMON
BURGERS WITH EDAMAME BEAN SALAD

 MAKES: 4

SE E SOY F G SF DF NF

For the burgers
4 small wild salmon fillets, skin removed
Zest of 2 limes
1 handful of fresh coriander
2 spring onions, roughly chopped
2 red chillies, deseeded and roughly chopped
1 egg
1 thumb-sized piece of fresh root ginger, peeled and roughly chopped
1 tablespoon rapeseed oil, plus extra for greasing the tray
1 tablespoon wholegrain spelt flour

For the salad
3 courgettes
A handful of baby spinach
180g edamame beans
10 runner beans, finely sliced
1 red pepper, finely sliced

For the dressing
Juice of 1 lemon
1 spring onion, very finely chopped
½ red chilli, very finely chopped
1 clove of garlic, very finely chopped
1 thumb-sized piece of fresh root ginger, peeled and grated
1 teaspoon toasted sesame oil
½ teaspoon Himalayan fine rock salt

I find that wild salmon is an all round 'clean' fish. I usually find wild salmon in the freezer of my local supermarket or I use the canned wild salmon from the health-food shop. Salmon is complete 'brain fuel'. It has very high levels of omega-3 fatty acids, which are beneficial for memory and overall brain health. This dish is ideal for a weekend brunch, lunch or dinner. High in protein, essential fats, dietary fibre and vitamin C. Low GL.

Preheat your grill to a medium heat. Lightly grease a baking tray.

To make the burgers, finely dice the salmon fillets and place them in a bowl. Place the rest of the ingredients except for the flour in a blender and blitz to a rough paste. Add this to the salmon and mix well, then add the flour and mix it through. Form into four patties and place on the greased baking tray. Place under the grill to cook the burgers for 12 minutes on each side, until golden.

Meanwhile, to prepare the salad, either slice your courgettes finely or use a peeler to create thin strips. Place the courgette noodles in a large bowl and add the baby spinach, edamame beans, runner beans and red pepper.

To make the dressing, combine all the ingredients together.

To serve, simply drizzle the dressing over the salad and serve with the hot salmon burgers.

SPICY MANGO
COCONUT FISH DISH

SERVES: 3

Ingredients

2 tablespoons coconut oil
500g fresh fish fillets (monkfish, salmon, whiting or hake, or this recipe can be made with chicken or prawns)
1 teaspoon paprika
1 teaspoon ground turmeric
1 teaspoon cayenne pepper
Pinch of Himalayan fine rock salt
1 large onion, diced
2 cloves of garlic, minced
300ml water or gluten-free fish stock
2 tablespoons creamed coconut or natural coconut yoghurt
100g mangetout
100g broccoli florets
50g fresh mango, chopped
2 tablespoons mango chutney
Cooked short-grain brown rice, to serve

Foods like garlic, onions, coconut oil, apple cider vinegar, camomile, lavender, ginger, lemons and cayenne pepper will help your body rid itself of excess yeast. Coconut's medium-chain fats are easily absorbed and are used as an energy source, which increases the body's metabolism. Always use your coconut oil within a month for the best freshness. High in essential fats, protein, calcium and dietary fibre.

Heat the coconut oil in a wok set over a low to medium heat. Season the fish with the paprika, turmeric, cayenne and some salt and lightly brown the fillets in the wok. Remove and set aside to cool, then dice the fish into large cubes.

Add the onion, garlic, water or fish stock and the creamed coconut to the wok. Bring to a boil, then reduce the heat and simmer for about 10 minutes, until slightly thickened. Add the fish, mangetout, broccoli, fresh mango and mango chutney. Cover the wok and cook for an additional 5 minutes.

Serve with short-grain brown rice and enjoy.

SNACKS AND DESSERTS

Done right, snacking can help you control your overall calorie intake for the day by keeping your hunger in check. However, many snack foods are high in fat and sugar and don't offer enough protein to satisfy hunger. A healthy snack combines some carbohydrate – in the form of whole grains, fruits or vegetables – with some protein.

Keep quick, easy snacks on hand to provide immediate energy between meals and while on the go. Simple snacks like apples and almond butter provide both carbohydrates and protein. Likewise, hummus on crackers or homemade energy bars and smoothies can be great boosters between meals.

MY FRUITOLOGY

AREN'T FRUITS FULL OF SUGAR?

I've been asked this question so many times! The fact is, this misunderstanding is holding athletes and everyday people across the country back from their health and performance potential, so it's time we clear up the confusion and get things back on track.

Firstly, when it comes to performance, health and convenience, fruits are in a league of their own. I often refer to them as nature's ultimate fast foods. After all, they pack in tons of benefits, including fibre (which helps clean our system in addition to keeping us feeling full), vitamins, minerals, healthy phytochemicals (which protect us on many levels) and lots of generally low-glycaemic carbohydrates (which means they don't spike your blood sugar – instead, they supply good-quality, slow-burning nutrients).

Secondly, our bodies need good-quality, slow-burning sugars (carbohydrates) every day. Our systems are built to run almost entirely on natural sugars (carbohydrates). Our body can even take protein (our muscle) and fat (body fat) and convert it to sugar (glucose) when we don't get enough carbohydrates in our diet.

So what's my rule of thumb on healthy fruit consumption? Eat one small piece of fruit with every meal. Pineapple or apple work best with dinner for digestion. Find yourself hungry in between meals? Grab a piece of fruit. Looking for a good mid-morning snack? Make or buy a quick fruit smoothie (see page 50). Know that you'll be doing your body and your performance a great service as you supply it with one of the best sources of nutrients you can find on store shelves.

SELECT STORES
FAMOUS SPIRULINA BARS

 MAKES: 12

Ingredients

450g unsalted butter

130g honey

70g peanut or almond butter

125g mixed seeds (we use a
mixture of sunflower, sesame
and poppy seeds)

2 teaspoons spirulina powder

625g oats (or gluten-free oats)

Oats are an excellent source of iron, magnesium and soluble fibre and are low in saturated fat and sodium. Eaten regularly, oats may also help to lower cholesterol.

Our famous Spirulina Bars were initially an idea put together by myself and local home baker Sue Hill. I then adapted it with friend and baker Jayne Courtney of Dalkey, who now has a successful gluten-free bakery, Gluttony, in Blackrock. We wanted to find a way to use the plant protein spirulina in baking, *et voilà*, here is the result. High in dietary fibre, protein and essential fats. Low GL.

Preheat the oven to 180°C/gas mark 4/350°F. Line a 22cm x 32cm Swiss roll tin with parchment paper.

Melt the butter, honey and peanut or almond butter in a large pot, then stir in the seeds and spirulina powder. Remove the pot from the heat and stir in the oats, making sure that they are all coated with the wet ingredients.

Spread the mixture into the prepared tin and bake for 20–25 minutes, until golden. Cut into squares while they are still warm (not hot!), but allow to cool completely before removing from the tin.

SEEDY MANGO
AND DATE ENERGY BARS

 MAKES: 9

Ingredients

80g coconut oil or butter, plus
extra for greasing

80g brown rice syrup

80g Medjool dates, stoned and
finely chopped

50g dark tahini (or you can use a
pumpkin seed spread or peanut
butter)

120g rolled oats (you can also
use quinoa flakes)

80g chopped hazelnuts

50g dried mango

40g pumpkin seeds

40g sesame seeds

40g sunflower seeds

20g ground flaxseeds

These satisfying homemade energy bars were developed by my friend, work colleague, home baker and nutritional coach Eleanor Hagan. These are fantastic for adults' and kids' lunchboxes – just don't let your mates know or there will be none left for you come lunchtime. High in vitamin E, zinc, dietary fibre, plant protein and essential fats. Low GL.

Preheat the oven to 180°C/gas mark 4/350°F. Lightly grease a 20cm square tin and line the base with baking parchment.

In a small saucepan set over a medium heat, melt together the coconut oil or butter, brown rice syrup, chopped dates and tahini. Stir constantly until smooth and thick.

Combine the oats, hazelnuts, mango and seeds in a large bowl. Pour in the melted coconut mixture and stir well to combine.

Spoon the mixture into the prepared tin and press it down firmly and evenly with the back of a spoon. Bake for about 20 minutes, until lightly golden on top.

Leave to cool, then slice into bars or squares. Eat straight away or store in an airtight container in the fridge for up to ten days.

LUNCHBOX
ENERGY BARS

 MAKES: 12

Ingredients

210g oats

80g blueberries

75g almonds

60g pistachios

40g ground flaxseeds

40g walnuts

25g pumpkin seeds

25g sunflower seeds

120g honey

90g apple sauce

225g almond butter

You can buy the best apple sauces in health-food shops or wholefood stores. My favourite ones are the organic apple sauces, as they have more flavour. Obviously you can make your own apple sauce too – I usually use the apple pulp that's left over when I juice apples. Just add it to a small bowl of water and add lemon juice and a tablespoon of honey, then pour it into a small pot and simmer for 8 minutes on a low heat while stirring. High in dietary fibre, plant protein and essential fats. Low GL.

Line a 22cm x 32cm baking tin with parchment paper. Using a wooden spoon or your clean hands, mix all of the dry ingredients together in a bowl. Add the honey and apple sauce and mix again, then mix in the almond butter.

Spread the mixture as evenly as possible in the baking tin and put in the freezer for approximately 1 hour, until frozen and set. Remove the slab of bars by lifting the parchment paper out of the tin. Cut into twelve bars.

Store in a freezer bag or a glass container in the freezer. They stay fresh once they are well sealed for up to a few weeks.

BLUEBERRY
AND VANILLA SPELT MUFFINS

 MAKES: 12

Ingredients

300g white spelt flour

2 teaspoons baking powder

½ teaspoon Himalayan fine rock salt

80g honey or agave syrup

2 eggs, beaten

70g unsalted butter, melted

200ml oat milk

1 teaspoon vanilla essence

200g blueberries

I wash the blueberries just before I use them so I don't lose the blue hue that protects the skin's surface. Blueberries have compounds similar to those found in cranberries that may help prevent urinary tract infections. High in protein, dietary fibre and vitamin C. Low GL.

Preheat the oven to 220°C/gas mark 7/425°F. Line a 12-hole muffin tin with paper cases.

Sieve the flour, baking powder and salt into a large bowl and mix in the honey or syrup.

In a separate bowl, mix together the beaten eggs, melted butter, oat milk and vanilla essence. Stir the liquid ingredients into the dry, then fold in the blueberries.

Spoon the batter into the muffin cases and bake for 15–20 minutes, until a skewer inserted into the centre of a muffin comes out clean. Leave to cool on a wire rack.

FULL-ON FIG,

CRANBERRY AND OAT BRAN MUFFINS

🍴 **MAKES: 12**

Ingredients

150g oat bran

30g bran flakes

120ml apple juice

150g dried figs, finely chopped

100g dried cranberries

1 large banana, mashed

1 egg, beaten

230ml apple juice concentrate

120ml milk

3 tablespoons extra virgin olive oil

2 tablespoons honey

180g wholewheat spelt flour

90g rolled oats

2 teaspoons baking powder

1½ teaspoons baking soda

1 teaspoon ground cinnamon

Figs are an excellent source of fibre and are extremely alkaline, which makes them such an important 'big hug' food after an illness or if you are just out of hospital. High in dietary fibre, protein and essential fats.

Preheat the oven to 180°C/gas mark 4/350°F. Line a 12-hole muffin tin with paper cases.

Combine the oat bran and bran flakes in a large bowl with the apple juice, making sure to moisten the flakes evenly. Add the figs, cranberries, mashed banana, beaten egg, apple juice concentrate, milk, olive oil and honey, and mix well.

In a separate bowl, combine the flour, rolled oats, baking powder, baking soda and cinnamon. Add to the bran mixture and mix well.

Spoon the batter into the muffin cases. Bake for 20–25 minutes, until risen. Cool on a wire rack.

COCONUT
CRUNCHES

 MAKES: 12

Ingredients

170g pecans

170g almonds

2 tablespoons agave sugar

290g creamed coconut

1 tablespoon coconut oil

¼ teaspoon Himalayan fine rock
 salt

25g desiccated coconut, toasted

Perfect for a nibble or with your hot evening drink. Before you know it, you'll be acting the nut! You can find low GL agave sugar in your local health-food shop. High in essential fats, plant protein, dietary fibre, vitamin E and zinc. Low GL.

Preheat the oven to 150°C/gas mark 2/300°F.

Spread the nuts on a baking sheet and toast very lightly for 15 minutes.

Process the agave sugar in a food processor until it's very fine. Place the jar of creamed coconut in hot water to soften it. In a medium-sized bowl, beat the creamed coconut, coconut oil, agave sugar and salt with an electric mixer until creamy. Fold in the toasted nuts and mix well with a large spoon until all the nuts are well coated.

Line the baking sheet with parchment paper and spread out the nut mixture evenly. Sprinkle with the desiccated coconut and place the baking sheet in the refrigerator.

When cold, break into bite-size pieces. Store in an airtight container in the refrigerator for up to ten days.

FUEL FOOD

ENERGY BITES

 MAKES: 15

Ingredients

10 large unsulphured apricots

10 large, fresh Medjool dates,
 pitted and roughly chopped

240g ground almonds

240g almond butter

100g hemp protein

3 tablespoons cacao powder

100ml fresh apple juice

½ teaspoon ground nutmeg

Pinch of Himalayan fine rock salt

40g cocoa powder

40g desiccated coconut

Let's get energetic! These healthy sweet bites are winning simple snacks at our shop with children, parents and athletes for mental and physical performance. They only take a little time to whip up and they keep well in the fridge for up to ten days. They also freeze well. We use hemp protein, but you can add your favourite protein powder to this if you like. High in plant protein, essential fats and dietary fibre. Low GL.

Soak the apricots in a small bowl of hot water for 15 minutes, then drain.

Add the apricots, chopped dates, ground almonds, almond butter, hemp protein, cacao powder, apple juice, nutmeg and salt to a food processor. Process until the mixture forms a ball. If the mixture is too wet, you can add some more ground almonds or some desiccated coconut. If it's too dry, add some more apple juice.

Form into fifteen golf ball-sized balls. Roll in some cocoa powder and desiccated coconut. You could also roll these energy bites in some sunflower or sesame seeds for extra va va voom. Refrigerate for a couple of hours before serving.

Keep the energy bites stored in an airtight container in the fridge, where they will last for up to ten days.

MAMA'S BLUEBERRY,
PEAR AND APPLE CRUMBLE

 SERVES: 6

Ingredients
300g blueberries
4 apples, cut into chunks
4 pears, cut into chunks
1 tablespoon freshly squeezed
 lemon juice
Small pinch of Himalayan fine
 rock salt
120g dark brown sugar
90g brown rice flour
70g unsalted butter, diced
60g oat flakes (or millet flakes for
 a gluten-free option)
½ teaspoon ground cinnamon

Blueberries have the highest amount of antioxidants of any fruit, which makes them very powerful for immune health. High in vitamin C and dietary fibre.

Preheat the oven to 200°C/gas mark 6/400°F.

Combine the fruit, lemon juice and a small pinch of salt in a large bowl, then spoon into a medium-sized baking dish.

Pulse the remaining ingredients in a food processor until they resemble coarse breadcrumbs and cover the fruit with the crumble topping.

Place in the oven and bake for 30 minutes, until the top has browned and the fruit is bubbling. This crumble can be served hot or at room temperature. It goes very well with ice cream, coconut ice cream or smooth almond butter.

ALMOND BUTTER
CHOCOLATE MOUSSE

 SERVES: 3

Ingredients

3 ripe avocados, stoned and
  peeled
120g cacao powder
160ml maple syrup
120ml water
Pinch of ground cinnamon
1 teaspoon natural vanilla
  essence
160g crunchy almond butter with
  no oil
6 fresh Medjool dates, pitted and
  roughly chopped
½–1 teaspoon vanilla essence
Small pinch of Himalayan fine
  rock salt

More and more health experts are recognising that avocados are vital and recommend eating some every day! This angelic mousse is the perfect dessert to make any dinner party a triumph. It's also vegan, light and satisfying, making it a champion for any sweet tooth fixation. High in vitamin E, dietary fibre, essential fats and plant protein. Low GL.

To make the mousse, put everything into a food processor and blend it all up. Add more water if required to create a smooth, velvety, mousse-like texture.

Pour or spoon the mixture evenly into three wide whiskey glasses and put in the fridge for 1 hour before serving.

These will keep in the fridge for up to five days when placed in an airtight container. This mousse is delicious served with some fresh berries.

CHIA OVERNIGHT MOUSSE
WITH ALMOND AND COCONUT

 SERVES: 2

Ingredients
100g ripe banana, peeled and
 mashed
470ml coconut drinking milk
2 tablespoons almond butter
1 teaspoon vanilla extract
½ teaspoon ground cinnamon
180g chia seeds

Chia seeds are high in omega-3 essential fats, a deficiency of which may cause depression and insomnia. The better your blood levels of omega-3 fats, the better your levels of serotonin, the 'happy hormone', are likely to be. High in plant protein, dietary fibre, essential fats, calcium and iron.

Blend the banana, coconut milk, almond butter, vanilla extract and cinnamon in a high-speed blender for 5 seconds. Transfer to two glass jars and stir in the chia seeds, dividing the seeds evenly between the two jars. Seal the jars, put in the fridge and leave overnight. By morning, the pudding will be set as the chia seeds will have soaked up the milk and become jelly-like.

Enjoy with seasonal fruit and/or berries, toasted coconut flakes, ground flaxseeds and a drizzle of honey if you like it sweet. It's handy to have as a healthy go-to snack at work or in the evening. This will keep for three days in the fridge.

NAUGHTY GLUTEN-FREE
MOROCCAN ORANGE CAKE

🍴 SERVES: 8

Ingredients
200g dark brown sugar
4 eggs, separated
Zest of 2 oranges
Juice of 1 orange
200g ground almonds

For the syrup glaze
130g caster sugar
Juice of 2 oranges
1 cinnamon stick
1 teaspoon orange essence or
 Cointreau

This recipe was developed by my friend and gluten-free work colleague, Eleanor Hickson, from Killiskey Bakery in the Garden of Wicklow. High in vitamin C, vitamin E, dietary fibre and protein.

Preheat the oven to 180°C/gas mark 4/350°F.

Line a 22cm or 23cm round cake tin with parchment paper.

Beat the brown sugar, egg yolks, orange zest and juice in a large mixing bowl until fluffy and yellow. Gradually beat in the ground almonds.

In a separate spotlessly clean, dry bowl, beat the egg whites until soft peaks form. Gently fold the egg whites into the cake batter with a metal spoon. Spoon the batter into the lined cake tin. Bake for 40 minutes, until a toothpick inserted into the centre comes out clean and the cake is golden brown. Leave to rest on a wire rack in the tin until it's cool.

To make the glaze, simmer the caster sugar, orange juice and cinnamon stick in a saucepan for 5 minutes, until the sugar has dissolved. Remove from the heat and allow to cool, then add the orange essence or Cointreau. Pour the syrup over the lukewarm cake in its tin.

Serve with vanilla ice cream or natural yoghurt.

SPELT
AND ALMOND LEMON LOAF

🍴 **MAKES: 2 LOAF CAKES**

Ingredients
350g + 3 heaped tablespoons
  caster sugar
350g unsalted butter, softened
Zest and juice of 4 lemons
6 large eggs
200g white spelt flour
150g almond flour or ground
  almonds

I've had the opportunity to work with amazing bakers over the years. My friend and work colleague Adrienne Byron is a truly inspirational spelt baker and this is our favourite moist, zesty loaf of hers that we would like to share with you. This loaf cake freezes very well, either as a full loaf or as slices. Enjoy! High in vitamin C, vitamin E, essential fats, dietary fibre and protein.

Preheat the oven to 170°C/gas mark 3/325°F.

Line two 2lb loaf tins with parchment paper.

Put 350g of sugar, the butter and the lemon zest in a mixing bowl. Beat until it is light and fluffy using a hand-held mixer or a free-standing one. Add in the eggs one at a time. If you think the batter is starting to curdle, add a tablespoon of the almond flour. Gently fold in the spelt flour and almond flour until just combined. Divide the batter between the two lined tins.

Bake for approximately 40 minutes, until a skewer inserted into the centre of the loaf comes out clean.

Meanwhile, pour the lemon juice into a saucepan and add the remaining 3 heaped tablespoons of caster sugar. Simmer until the sugar has dissolved.

When the lemon loaves come out of the oven, pour the syrup onto the cakes and leave them to cool in their tins. When they are cold, turn them out onto a rack and slice each loaf into eight or ten pieces.

HILARY'S SWEET POTATO
AND CRANBERRY BROWNIES

🍴 **MAKES: 18**

Ingredients

2 medium sweet potatoes, peeled and cut into large cubes

4 large eggs, beaten

90ml maple syrup

90ml date syrup

1 teaspoon vanilla paste

1 tablespoon vanilla essence

90ml coconut oil

100g ground almonds

60g cocoa powder

50g cacao powder

1 teaspoon gluten-free baking powder

1 teaspoon Himalayan fine rock salt

70g dried cranberries

Bee pollen, to decorate

Cocoa and cacao powder provide all of the health benefits of chocolate without the calories from added sugars. These powders offer double the amount of antioxidants as a bar of dark chocolate and as much fibre as most fruits and vegetables. Cocoa and cacao powder are also a rich source of many essential minerals, including magnesium, copper and iron. These brownies are made by my sister Hilary every day at Select Stores. They're a real crowd pleaser. High in vitamin C, vitamin E, dietary fibre, essential fats and protein. Low GL.

Preheat the oven to 180°C/gas mark 4/350°F.

Grease a 20cm x 30cm baking tin.

Boil the sweet potatoes in a saucepan of salted water for 30 minutes, until soft. Drain the water off and mash the sweet potatoes.

Mix the mashed sweet potato, eggs, maple syrup, date syrup, vanilla paste and vanilla essence in a large bowl. Add in the coconut oil while mixing.

In another bowl, mix together the ground almonds, cocoa and cacao powders, baking powder and salt. Add this dry mix to the bowl of wet ingredients and stir until it's all blended well. Mix in the cranberries, then pour the batter into the greased baking tin.

Bake in the oven for 20 minutes. Check the brownies with a knife inserted into the centre – if it comes out dry they are ready to rock and roll. Remove from the oven and cool on a wire rack, then cut into eighteen squares. Scatter with some bee pollen to make them look even prettier.

INDEX

MERCIER PRESS
Cork
www.mercierpress.ie

© Oliver McCabe, 2016

© Images of Dalkey: Linda O'Reilly (p. 8); Colm Murphy (p. 13); John Fahy (pp. 114–15); Terry McDonagh (pp. 188–9, 255 and endpapers), 2016

ISBN: 978 1 78117 366 4

10 9 8 7 6 5 4 3 2 1

A CIP record for this title is available from the British Library

Photography by Rob Kerkvliet, A Fox In The Kitchen, www.afoxinthekitchen.com

Styled by Orla Neligan of Cornershop Productions, www.cornershopproductions.com

Assisted by Susie Coakley

PROPS

Avoca: HQ Kilmacanogue, Bray, Co. Wicklow. T: (01) 2746939; E: info@avoca.ie; W: www.avoca.ie

Meadows & Byrne: Dublin, Cork, Galway, Clare, Tipperary. T: (01) 2804554/(021) 4344100;
E: info@meadowsandbyrne.ie; W: www.meadowsandbyrne.com

Marks & Spencer: Unit 1–28, Dundrum Town Centre, Dublin 16. T: 01 299 1300; W: www.marksandspencer.ie

Article Dublin: Powerscourt Townhouse, South William Street, Dublin 2. T: 01 6799268;
E: items@articledublin.com; W: www.articledublin.com

Dunnes Stores: 46–50 South Great Georges Street, Dublin 2. T: 1890 253185; W: www.dunnesstores.com

Harold's Bazaar: 208 Harold's Cross Road, Dublin 6W. T: 087 7228789

Historic Interiors: Oberstown, Lusk, Co. Dublin. T: 01 8437174; E: killian@historicinteriors.net

TK Maxx: The Park, Carrickmines, Dublin 18. T: 01 2074798; W: www.tkmaxx.ie

Baker's Bling on Etsy: W: www.etsy.com/shop/BakersBlingShop

Fired Earth: 19 George's Street Lower, Co. Dublin. T: (01) 6636160; www.firedearth.com

Tiger Stores: T: 01 598 8800; W: www.tiger-stores.ie

Golden Biscotti ceramics: W: http://goldenbiscotti.bigcartel.com

The Patio Centre: The Hill Centre, Johnstown Road, Glenageary, Cabinteely, Dublin 18. T: 01 2350714;
W: www.thepatiocentre.com

Industry Design: 41 A/B Drury Street, Dublin 2. T: 01 6139111; W: www.industrydesign.ie

Printed and bound in the EU.